TELL ME: Children, Reading & Talk
with THE READING ENVIRONMENT

Since first publication *The Reading Environment* (1991) and the influential *Tell Me: Children, Reading & Talk* (1993) have been continuously in print and are often used together. They have been published in North American and Australian editions and, unusually for UK books about reading and education, in nine foreign-language editions.

Now that *The Reading Environment* has been updated in time for its twentieth anniversary, and the text for both books revised and reset, the connections between them are emphasized and enhanced by their presentation in a single volume.

BY THE SAME AUTHOR

Breaktime
Dance on My Grave
Now I Know
The Toll Bridge
Postcards from No Man's Land
(*recipient 1999 Carnegie Medal; 2003 Michael L. Printz Award*)
This is All: The Pillow Book of Cordelia Kenn
Seal Secret
The Present Takers
(*all Bodley Head*)

Booktalk: Occasional Writing on Literature and Children
Reading Talk
(*both Thimble Press*)

In 2002 the Hans Christian Andersen Medal was awarded to Aidan Chambers, who was elected a Fellow of The Royal Society of Literature in 2009.

Aidan Chambers

Tell Me

Children, Reading and Talk

with

The Reading Environment

The Thimble Press

Cover: Ted van Lieshout

ISBN 978-0903355-54-4

Combined volume first published 2011 by
THE THIMBLE PRESS
Lockwood, Station Road, Woodchester
Stroud, Glos. GL5 5EQ. UK
www.thimblepress.co.uk

Printed by Lightning Source

CONTENTS

Part One
The Reading Environment

PART TWO

TELL ME

PART ONE

THE READING ENVIRONMENT

1

Introduction

All reading has to happen somewhere.

And every reader knows that where we read affects how we read: with what pleasure and willingness and concentration. Reading in bed, feeling warm and comfortable and relaxed, is different from reading on a cold railway station waiting for a train, or in the sun on a crowded beach, or in a library full of other readers, or alone in a favourite chair at ten o'clock in the morning.

But it isn't only a matter of place – of setting. It is also a matter of having the books we want, and the mood we're in, and the time we've got, and whether we're interrupted. Not to mention our general attitude to reading (whether or not it is something we enjoy for its own sake) and why, particularly, we are reading at that moment (as a work duty or for private pleasure).

These are some of the things that influence us. They make up the social context of reading. Taken together they form what I call the reading environment. Part One of this book describes its main features, dealing with them one by one, though in fact they are inseparable and interact with each other.

If we want to be skilful in helping other people, especially children, become willing, avid, and – most important of all – thoughtful readers, we need to know how to create a reading environment that enables them. This book is about that. And it is intended for people who work with children and reading – teachers, librarians, parents; those who want to refresh and revise their practice, and those just starting out who may be dealing with these things for the first time.

I begin by looking at what some people call 'the reading process' in order to identify the essential activities it involves. Not what goes on inside our heads – the province of reading experts – but what readers have to do to make 'reading' possible.

2

The Reading Circle

Every time we read we engage in a sequence of activities.

One activity leads to another. Not in a linear chain reaction, beginning at point A and continuing to distant point Z, but more like a circle in which the sequence returns to the start again, so the beginning is always its end and the end its beginning.

A diagram of the reading circle looks like this:

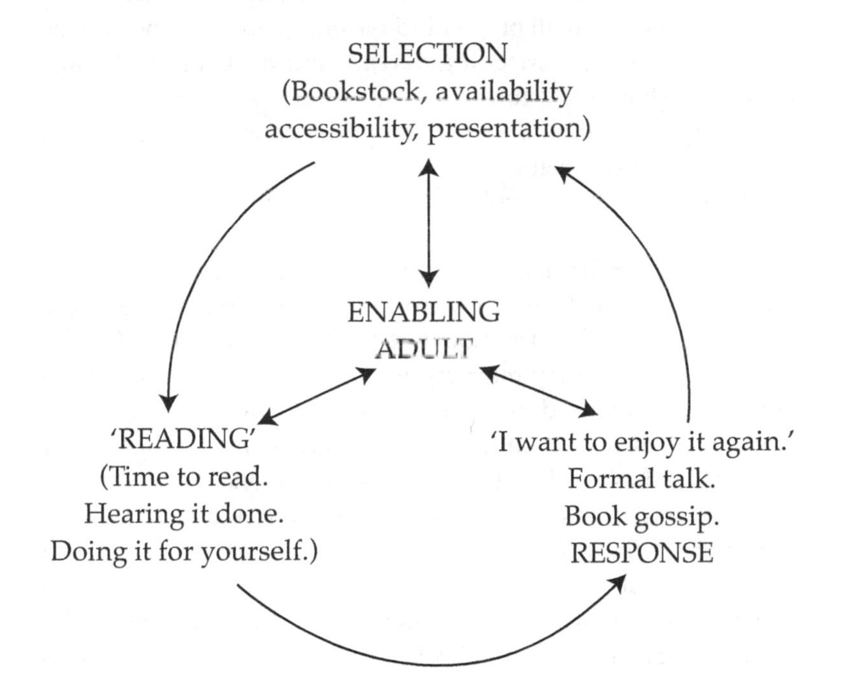

SELECTION

All reading begins with selection.

Every time we read we make a choice from all the print available to us – books, magazines, newspapers, ebooks, electronic texts, business documents, government forms, junk mail, advertisements, holiday brochures: a multitude of possibilities. This is true even when we are simply walking along the streets, which are full of 'environmental print' – road signs, posters, shop-front messages, graffiti. Out of all this clutter of letterforms, we pick what we want. If we're finding the way, for example, we're mainly interested in signs that tell us where to go next.

When choosing books, we are affected by all sorts of influences. I'll be discussing the ones that relate to reading literature in later chapters. What must be said here is that all selection depends on availability. If there are only a few books, the chances of finding one we want are smaller than if there are a great many. Even so, if the great many are of only one kind – only mystery stories, say, or novels about Argentina – and are a kind we don't like, we are less likely to choose any than when there are fewer books but all of the kind we enjoy. So books need to be available to us if we are going to read, and the book stock must include the kind we want.

Though I mention books, this applies to every kind of text, paper print or electronic.

Also, however, the books must be accessible.

For example: When I was nine, my school classroom contained about fifty storybooks. They were kept in a locked cupboard which was opened for a few minutes every Friday afternoon, when we were told to choose a book to take home for the weekend. On Monday morning we returned the books and the cupboard was locked again until the next Friday. All week the books were available, but they weren't accessible till the teacher opened the cupboard and allowed us to take one.

This may seem a pernickety distinction but it is very important. I know of a school with a very attractive-looking and well-stocked library, but the children are discouraged by the head teacher from using it because they might dirty the books. The library isn't really for them; it's there as a show-place to impress visitors. The books are available, but they certainly aren't accessible. I've also been into a classroom where there were plenty of books but the children were only allowed to look at them when they had done well in other work. In that case accessibility was a reward used to confirm the success of some children and the failure of others. It had very little to do with encouraging everyone to read.

However, selection doesn't only depend on being able to get our hands on books. How they are presented affects us too. We can be put off or attracted by the way they are displayed and shelved, a subject I'll deal with in Chapter 5. All I want to say here is this. One thing confident readers know is how to set about choosing what they want. They know how to browse and how to obtain information about books they can't find. They know how to make a bookstock work for them, be it a large or small public library, a bookshop, a classroom collection, or just a best friend's shelf of favourites. The same is true of electronic systems of provision.

Like everything else to do with reading, the way we learn best how to select confidently is to do it for ourselves, while an already confident, trusted reader is nearby to show how it is done and give help when needed.

'READING'

It is pointless to spend time selecting something to read if we never 'read' what we've selected.

I've put inverted commas round the word 'read' in order to emphasize that reading doesn't only mean passing our eyes over printed words in order to decipher them. Rather, as the reading circle reminds us, the reading process comprises a number of activities of which 'taking the words off the page' is only one.

The trouble is that English doesn't have a word other than 'reading' for the time spent looking at words on a page. And this has an unfortunate result. It often leads learning readers to believe they haven't succeeded until they are able to decipher the printed words in a book. Whereas, of course, they are succeeding from the moment they pick up a book and pay attention to it. A preschool child who cannot yet 'read', but who looks at Eric Hill's *Where's Spot?* and begins to sort out which way up it must be held, and how the pages turn, and what to do with the flaps, and enjoys all this so much she finds someone who can read the words aloud while she looks at the pictures, is being as successful at that moment in her reading life as is an academic critic busy sorting out the verbal puzzles in James Joyce's *Ulysses*.

We best help learning readers when we confirm their successes as they move round the reading circle. Going to look at a collection of books is a success. Picking out a book is a success. Deciding whether to give it more attention, or to reject it in favour of another, is a success. Settling down to 'read' is a success. And so on.

TIME

Another of the most important truths about reading is that it takes time. We read some messages, like familiar signs, so quickly we're hardly aware we're doing it. Certain kinds of print, like news items in tabloid newspapers, can be read very quickly, while we're doing other things and talking at the same time. But some books, especially works of literature, may not only take a long time to read but demand concentrated attention. More about this in Chapter 7.

Pleasure in a literary book comes from discovering the patterns of event, of character, of ideas, of image, of language woven into it. Books for very young children are designed with pictures and words that allow this discovery to take place in one reading of a few minutes' duration because for very young children a few minutes' sustained concentration is demanding. When they have enjoyed the experience a number of times they gradually learn what time and effort they must give in order to receive the return of pleasure that makes reading worth while. Margaret Meek has shown us 'how texts teach what readers learn'. Here, we are thinking about how adults can help learning readers to concentrate on the texts that teach them the most.

This process of building up pleasurable experience, and extending the length of time we can concentrate, depends on a regular giving of oneself to books that repay the effort. So providing time to read, and helping learner readers attend to rewarding books for longer and longer periods of time, are important aspects of an enabling adult's job.

PLACE

We 'read' best in surroundings that help concentration. For instance, some kinds of busy activity going on around us can be distracting. And usually it's hard to read when there's television nearby. At home we can hope to suit ourselves. But in school or playgroup or library or any other communally used space where lots of different people are engaged in many activities, it is necessary to manage things carefully so that all children have regular reading times and their concentration is protected. I discuss this in detail in Chapter 7.

RESPONSE

It is a fact of our psychological make-up that we cannot read anything without experiencing some kind of response.

Literary reading affects people in many ways. In everyday talk these reactions are described as pleasure, boredom, excitement, interest, enjoyment – even using, if you're like the French critic Roland Barthes, the partly sexual word *jouissance* (joy, bliss, ecstasy) for the greatest reading pleasure of all.

Two responses are important in helping children become more thoughtful readers.

The first is that, having enjoyed a book, we want to experience the same pleasure again. This may be expressed as a desire to reread the book, or to read others by the same writer, or more books of the same kind, or simply to read for the sake of the activity itself. Thus we feel compelled to make another selection, and we start round the reading circle again.

The second response is that we can't help talking about it to someone else. We want other people, especially our friends, to experience it too. We want to explore what has happened to us and sort out what the book has meant and why it is important to us.

Booktalk takes two forms.

One is informal gossip, the kind of chat that goes on between friends.

The other is more formal, more considered, the sort of discussion that goes on in classrooms or seminars.

Both kinds of talk tend to take us back into the reading circle. We want to read what our friends have found enjoyable, and we want to reread books that seriously interest us. And both kinds of talk may have another effect. They may help change the reading circle into a spiral.

Here is what I mean. I said earlier that my main interest is in helping people become thoughtful readers. It is quite easy to find avid readers who choose books often, read every day, even talk about how much they like it. But their main enjoyment seems to come from the fact that reading, for them, is a pleasant way of passing the time. They might as well be doing something else. What they certainly do not want is to be disturbed by what they read, or challenged, or made to 'sit up and think'. Often they are people who only ever read in bed at night in order to put themselves to sleep.

I must confess that I'm not very interested in reading as a soporific or as a pastime hobby. Children will do this anyway. Reading, for me, is a means of thought. One way of saying this is that literature gives us images to think with. Or, to use David Krech's word, literature gives us images to *perfink* (perceive, feel, think) with. C. S. Lewis put it another way. When reading literature, he said, we become a thousand different people and yet remain ourselves. Richard Hoggart wrote that he valued literature 'because of the way – the peculiar way – in which it explores, re-creates and seeks for meanings in human experience; because it explores the diversity, complexity and strangeness of that experience.' In literature, he added, we look at life 'with all the vulnerability, honesty, and penetration' we can command. Or we do if we read thoughtfully.

How do people become thoughtful readers? How do they shift from being pastime consumers of print into being attentive readers of literature?

My experience as a reader and as a teacher tells me that one of the answers lies in the kind of talk people do about their reading. Some kinds of talk, because they cause us to think more carefully, more deeply about what we've read, have the effect of making us more aware of what is happening to us. And this in turn makes us more discriminating in our selection.

So we break out of a limited, flat-earth view of reading, in which we only ever read the kinds of books that are familiar to us, and discover that the reading world is not flat but round, with many other interesting continents on it. Even more, that we can leave the world, which itself is small, and take off, spiralling up into a galaxy of other worlds, until eventually we can roam through the entire universe of literature, stopping wherever we want and exploring whichever strange planet takes our fancy.

But we only learn how to break free, only learn how to navigate round the reading circle in the first place, if we have the help of someone who already knows how to do it. I describe this kind of talk in detail in Part Two.

THE ENABLING ADULT

All other obstacles in the way of learner readers can be overcome if they have the help and example of a trusted, experienced adult reader. Any committed reader who has come from a non-reading, book-deprived background knows that, which is why I've placed an enabling adult at the centre of the reading circle. Yes, all learner readers help each other too, a topic discussed in Chapter 13. The two-directional arrows in the reading circle diagram are there to remind us that enablers also learn from those they help. Nevertheless, however helpful learners are to each other, in the end they depend on knowledgeable grownups because there are some things about every craft and every art – reading is both art and craft – that you only know from experience and can only be passed on by those who've learned them by experience.

3

The Set and the Setting

Two conditions influence the outcome of every human activity, helping to determine whether it is enjoyable or not, be the activity public or private, gregarious or solitary, formal or informal. Borrowing terms from the psychologists, I call them 'the set' and 'the setting'.

By 'the set' I mean that mix of mental and emotional attitudes we bring to the things we do. Our expectations, previous experience and knowledge, our present mood, our relationship with other participants, even the time of day and the weather: all these factors determine the way we behave.

By 'the setting' I mean the physical surroundings, and their appropriateness or otherwise to the activity in which we're involved.

Thus a picnic can be a disaster if one dominant member of the party is set against it – is feeling bad-tempered perhaps because he is there against his wishes and generally hates picnics anyway. And no matter how willing everyone may be to have a good time, it is difficult to do more than make the cheerful best of it if the picnic is held, by some bizarre accident of circumstance, near a stinking garbage dump in pouring rain: the setting isn't favourable.

On the other hand, people who are passionately devoted to a hobby or sport will endure without complaint conditions which would be unbearable to less ardent folk. So we see extraordinary hardships cheerfully borne – indeed, apparently enjoyed – by zealous climbers on icy mountains, by earnest single-handed sailors floating alone around the world, and by fishing hobbyists who weekend after weekend sit patiently on the banks of rivers, undeterred by the foulness of the weather and the small size of their catches.

Set, it seems, is a more powerful influence than setting

Reading is no different in this respect from any other activity. If we read willingly, expecting pleasure, we are likely to find enjoyment. If we are forced to read as a duty, expecting no delight, we are likely to find it a boring business. Settle down somewhere comfortable, and we can sometimes read happily for a long time. But if we don't feel comfortable and are bothered by numerous distractions, any but the most determined reader is likely to give up quite soon.

Obviously, therefore, we must remember that the set of both the teacher and the pupil towards reading will have a very strong influence on the outcome. And because setting can change a set of mind, swaying it for or against an activity, it is important to consider how each feature of the reading environment may affect the set of the people it is intended to support.

4

Reading Areas

Human beings are territorial animals, and they are ritualists.

We like to know what may be done where, when, how, and by whom. We need and respect places set aside for a particular purpose. And we like to know how we are meant to behave in different circumstances. So we are taught as children what kinds of behaviour are appropriate for different settings: when we are in the house of a stranger, for instance, or in a shop, or in a library, or at a football match, or at a birthday party. The best example of this is how all but a few people become quietly solemn when they enter a religious building, even though they may be quite unreligious themselves. It seems that our minds adapt to the kind of place we are in, as soon as we recognize our surroundings.

'Reading' is like that. It is an activity that has special behavioural needs. We have to set our minds right to do it – to concentrate on the book so that we are drawn inside it and give it our attention. Experience has proved how much it helps children to do this if places are set aside for reading only: places many teachers call 'reading areas'.

In classrooms, the reading area is most often a corner of the room. Cushions, or beanbags, soft furniture of that kind, make the area feel comfortable and inviting.

Some schools are lucky enough to have separate reading rooms as well, elaborate versions of reading corners, with space for displays of books you can look at and read while you're there. Because they are big enough for large groups or even a whole class, they are sometimes used for special book occasions as, for example, when a visiting author gives a talk or a schools service librarian comes to do a storytelling session.

For everyday use, the rules are quite simple. You go into the reading area to read quietly and for nothing else. And you don't distract other readers by talking to them or by moving about a lot.

Perhaps it's worth emphasizing that reading areas are not libraries where book stocks are kept, because people need to talk and write and move about when they are browsing, or finding books and borrowing them, or checking references.

Reading areas also signify value. You don't devote a place solely to one special activity unless you believe it to be enormously important. Just by being there, used in a certain way and protected by simple, reasonable rules, a reading area announces to pupils, without the teacher having to say anything about it, that in this classroom, this school, this community, reading is understood to be an essential occupation.

5

Displays

Book displays make books prominent.

They stimulate interest. They are decorative. They deeply influence the mental set of people who see them. Displays are, therefore, essential to an effective reading environment.

Putting books on show is also an important way of making recommendations by remote control. One adult can work closely with only a few children. In a large school we may never even pass the time of day with the majority. Through displays we can reach out to many more, both to those we know and those we don't.

Besides, there are times when some children don't much like us, however hard we try. Their dislike can carry over into the activities we are associated with. Then they won't read books we are seen to recommend. Displays get us out of the way. No one spends much time wondering who put them up before being attracted to whatever is on show.

Books on display speak for themselves. How well they do this depends on how well the display is presented, and how interesting the books' covers are. All in all, good displays take relatively little time and effort to set up compared with the value of their effect.

Good displays depend on two main ingredients:

- Astute selection of the books.
- An arrangement designed to attract children so that they will want to know more about the books.

The point to keep in mind is that displays work through visual appeal.

Other points to remember:

1. CHOICE OF SITE

A display set up in a dark corner of a busy corridor is not likely to receive much attention. Be sure there's room for people to stand and look without obstructing passers-by. There should be plenty of light, with, if possible, some highlighting, perhaps from a small spot.

2. APPEAL

We can learn a lot from good shop-window and museum displays about such things as grouping books, the kind of materials suitable for backgrounds, the use of space, different levels and massing of shapes, how to handle display lettering and captions. Avoid anything tatty or sloppily makeshift. Think carefully about the number of books included. Clutter is ugly, and overcrowding confuses the eye.

3. INITIAL IMPACT

Every display needs one feature which has an immediate, eye-catching effect, and other features (the books preferably) which hold people's interest once caught.

But every display has a natural life-span. As soon as it has become familiar, people cease to notice it. In a stable community like a school, judging when a display has reached its end is fairly easy: you simply keep an eye on how often it is looked at and how much interest it generates. Once this begins to flag, it's time to make a change.

4. MAINTENANCE

Open displays, as opposed to those behind glass or out of touching range, need frequent maintenance. Books and loose objects get displaced. Decorations get marked and damaged. Soon what began as an immaculately presented show looks tired and messy.

5. BOOKS

Copies of books on display ought, if possible, to be available for borrowing or buying. Readers are impatient. When they see a book that excites them, they want it then and there. The longer the time spent obtaining a book the more likely it is that interest will fade.

Recently a teacher told me about setting up a book display in the entrance hall of the school where she had just started work, which had a very poor reading environment. Next morning, during assembly, she talked about the display and the books in it, explaining that people could write their names on a sheet of paper beside the display, together with the titles of any books they wanted to read after the display was taken down. Assembly over, the children went to their classrooms. The teacher waited behind, talking to the head teacher. When she left to go to her own class, she passed the display. There wasn't a book on it. Every single one had been taken within two or three minutes of the end of assembly.

This anecdote illustrates several things:

- The grabby nature of determined readers.
- The effect of a good teacher talking about books.
- The thirst for reading in ordinary children who had been deprived – and who were said by the adults who had taught them till then to be uninterested in reading.
- And an instance, by the way, of books being available (as they are in any display) but not accessible (they weren't intended for borrowing while on display).

All displays pose the dilemma of creating a demand that sometimes can't be satisfied immediately. Another element, this, in deciding the useful life-span of a display. Some are set up with a life-span intended to be no longer than 'see-it, want-it, take-it'. Others have a publicly stated embargo, such as 'Nothing to be borrowed until Monday next'.

6. THEMES AND TOPICS

There are many variations on themes for displays. Here are some of the more common:

- New books. Always popular. Everyone likes to see what's just arrived. The problem is that everyone also wants to borrow them at once.
- Books sharing a link – novels about the sea, stories about dogs, picture books that use the comic-strip mode, a number of versions of the same folk tale, and so on.
- This week's author. Always popular and one of the best ways of drawing children's attention to writing they may not have tried and making them aware of authors.
- This week's artist or illustrator. As above but for deepening understanding of the visual aspects of a book.
- A selection in celebration of a topical occasion or an exploit in the news.
- Books produced by the same publisher, or in a series, or with some other shared book-production feature.
- Award-winning books.
- Books translated from other languages. On the whole, our children are ignorant of the literature of other languages and cultures. Focusing attention on books from other nationalities helps improve this situation.
- Books of film, TV and radio adaptations.
- Books reviewed by pupils in the school.
- Books accompanied by work done by pupils in response to their reading – drawings, stories, poems, models, book jackets, illustrations.
- 'Our Favourites.' Each class, or any group of pupils you care to put together, take it in turn to select their current favourites and devise a way of displaying them. Always popular. Sometimes controversial.

7. EXHIBITIONS

So far I've been talking about small-scale short-time displays. Now and then – say, twice a year – it's a good idea to put on a much bigger show, with many more books and elaborate backgrounds which most if not all the school can help create. Parents are invited to help and to view the books. Children's work is shown. They present a play or a poetry programme or some other event. Perhaps a reasonably well-known guest gives a talk, or a travelling company of actors or musicians gives a performance. Or the exhibition is used as a focus for discussing the school's policy on reading. Most of all, the occasion is a festive time, used to refresh interest and raise awareness.

The quality and kind of displays – or the absence of them – is another accurate indicator, I find, of the value placed on books and reading in a school. Every part of a building, in classrooms and outside them, should be examined as a possible display area. And just as with the management of the book stock itself, all kinds of people in partnership should be encouraged to arrange their own displays: teachers, teachers and pupils, pupils in various groupings, parents, parents and children, and so on. When this happens, making displays helps bind the community together as well as creating and encouraging readers.

6

Browsing

Regular readers know the pleasure of browsing.

They know that they may find just what they are looking for, but didn't know existed, among the piles of books on a second-hand bookstall, or when scanning the public library shelves more or less at random.

People do not become committed readers on a diet of prescribed texts only, however well chosen they may be. No one can be completely successful in selecting books for someone else. We all enjoy freedom of choice, and when we have freedom, our set of mind – our attitude – tends to be optimistic and positive. We cheerfully become willing readers when following our own instincts and tastes.

Like adults, children need opportunities to find for themselves the books that will satisfy their needs and suit their maturity and personality. Browsing offers that chance.

So time to browse is an important element in a reading environment, and it brings other advantages. Familiarity, for a start. People from 'non-book' homes (as I was) often feel that bookshops and large public libraries are forbidding places. All those shelves full of all those books. Where do you start? Browsing time provided in school, where there is a helpful adult already well known to the children, and classmates to talk to about what they've read and liked, can be the way many children discover how to choose books for themselves.

Then, working with children one-to-one is important. While a group of children browse the stock, the teacher can talk to them individually, encouraging and suggesting, informally listening to what each has to say.

At the same time, while picking and sampling, children can talk to each other, discussing the books they've read, swapping opinions, and egging their friends on to read the books they've enjoyed. The teacher may have said nothing, but by providing the right setting – an attractively arranged collection of books with space to move among them – and by allowing quiet talk, the teacher has helped the children to help each other. The peer group influence (see Chapter 13) has been put to work.

HOW MUCH BROWSING TIME AND WHEN?

In a well-managed classroom, there should be time for children to browse every day. A few minutes is long enough. When special exhibitions are on display, or when the class visits the school central collection, or when they go to the local public library, a longer period is necessary. Each of these has its own useful extent of time. The more to look at and the more special the occasion, the longer the time needed. Also, of course, the more careful must be the preparation of the children for what they are to see.

I've been talking about children browsing together in groups. But of course they browse on their own too. During school time, they fit it in between other jobs, which is not difficult if book stocks are available and accessible.

What it comes down to is this: there are formal and informal browsing times. During formal times children browse together, supervised by an adult. The purpose then may be to look carefully at a particular exhibition because we're studying something to do with it, or it may be simply to enjoy looking at books together as much as selecting some to read. The informal times, which may be in school hours or out of them, are when children browse on their own (though perhaps with a friend) because they want to enjoy books by themselves or because they need to find a book to read.

Unsupported by any other teaching, browsing is not enough to turn children into literate readers. The idea that all we have to do is surround children with books and everything else follows naturally is naive. Even if this were enough for some children, it certainly isn't enough for all. On the other hand, browsing is a much more important activity than its casual, apparently unstructured appearance may seem to an inexperienced eye. In fact, regular browsing is essential.

7

Reading Time

Being a reader means reading for yourself. All reading takes time.

If these propositions are true, another truth inevitably follows. Adults who care for children as readers must make sure that children have time to read for themselves.

Some years ago John Werner summarized the important features of Reading Time.

1. Each pupil must be given the opportunity to read, at her own speed, material of a difficulty suited to her. Some reading requires frequent practice.

2. No teacher can estimate which book will satisfy the intellectual and emotional needs of the individual. Therefore many books must be tried.

3. Such reading cannot be left to the pupil's leisure time. Many children come from homes where serious reading is simply not part of the way of life; TV and computers, DVDs and computer games, with all their advantages, have surely cut down the incentive to acquire the habit of reading seriously and at length where this is not already part of the accepted social pattern.

4. The teacher should not always be involved in the response to a book. Emotional blocks to reading can be formed by an unsatisfactory relationship with a teacher. With classes

of the size they are, it is not always possible for her to detect the problems soon enough. In any case, a previous teacher may have left the child with the legacy of an unsatisfactory attitude to reading.

5. A teacher cannot keep up with all the books from which a child's reading should be selected. If only directed reading is encouraged, the class will merely reflect the taste of the teacher rather than evolve their own.

6. If a child is reading only trash, then this fact should be taken into account and dealt with at other times.

7. Many of our major authors were nourished on an early diet of wide, random reading.

8. The child must learn to discriminate for himself. If a pupil is allowed to accept or reject, he will demand higher standards in reading material far sooner than if the teacher attempts to tell him what is good and what is bad.

Werner stresses that we need to read frequently and regularly during childhood and adolescence if we are to have the best chance of growing up as committed readers.

HOW OFTEN SHOULD CHILDREN READ FOR THEMSELVES?

Here is the optimum: Up to the age of sixteen every child should have an undirected, independent reading time every day during school hours. Wise parents will see that their children are encouraged to read for themselves, especially during weekends and school holidays.

HOW LONG SHOULD THESE TIMES BE?

The simple answer is: as long as a child can sustain concentration and interest, plus a little longer. But naturally, the length varies according to other limits. Very young children tend to have shorter attention spans than older children. Children who have grown up in a reading family and are used to 'giving themselves' to books can read for longer periods than children of the same age who come from non-reading families. Children in well-run, well-furnished classrooms can often concentrate for longer periods of time than those who are unlucky enough to be with an incompetent teacher (where the set is against it) or are housed in unattractive, uncomfortable rooms (where the setting doesn't help).

Nor can you expect a class of children who are not used to reading for themselves suddenly to do so just because a new teacher introduces a regular reading time. They must be prepared for it and perhaps even eased into it gradually. In these circumstances a good idea – when you have explained what is to happen and why – is to read aloud for a part of each session, because this draws people together and tunes their minds in to story. For the rest of the session the children read their own books for a period of time that is gradually lengthened as they get used to the activity and their reading stamina grows. Once they've become used to reading for themselves, they can get going without being read to first, and reading aloud can be given its own separate time.

USSR: UNINTERRUPTED SUSTAINED SILENT READING TIME

These times are for the period of reading.

And they are *uninterrupted*. They are not times when the teacher checks over pupils' work with them, or hears them read aloud, or bustles about the room doing odd jobs. In fact, working on the principle that children are more willing to do what is regarded as important by adults, the teacher should be reading herself at the same time.

Sustained reading happens best if we are confident that we won't be interrupted. But also there are moments when we need someone to encourage us. A teacher can provide the willpower that children sometimes lack to settle down and read. This is helped if a time is regularly set aside which everyone knows will be spent reading. A sacrosanct period is another of those rituals that condition our set of mind. Some schools do this all together at the same time. Others leave it up to class teachers to decide.

Silent? The older we get the more we tend to like to read in silence. Infant children often talk all the time they are reading. They point things out to each other, they laugh, they talk out the story, they criticize and extemporize. And they don't seem to be bothered by other children near them behaving in the same way. For them, an insistence on silence isn't necessary, might even turn them off reading. But by the age of eight children who have become willing readers quite understand that they should not interrupt other people during Reading Time and so this is a time for quiet.

I visited a class of nine-year-olds during their Reading Time the other day. Some were sitting alone at their work tables. Some were stretched out on the floor in the reading corner. A group of three boys was huddled round a table looking at a picture book and muttering about it together. There were twosomes silently reading from the same book. The room was not totally silent, but the sound was a murmur that disturbed no one. The teacher was reading a novel; every few minutes she would scan the room to check that all was well, and a couple of times in the twenty-five-minute session she walked around to see what was going on in the more obscure corners. Only once did she have to check a child who was in the opening moves of misbehaving. She did it by 'giving him a look', and when that seemed not to be enough, pointed a warning finger. He thought better of his plans, and went back to his book.

This was in March. The teacher had taken over that class the previous September. Before then they had been badly taught. They had not been given time to read for themselves, had not been given most of the advantages advocated in these pages. It had taken her three months – a term – to get them used to Reading Time. But by now, three months later, they would complain, she told me, if anything interfered with their daily session.

Here is another teacher's brief note on the results of starting a regular Reading Time during a year when he was trying to improve the reading environment in his two-class village school. He took the junior class, with children aged between eight and eleven:

> Private Silent Reading periods have been a success from the start. The younger ones kept to picture books and some didn't get into them, turning pages quickly and having big piles on the tables before them, sometimes being unwilling to share their personal store, but I hold this to be getting into the habit of using books and learning that it is an accepted social activity, surrounded as they are by books, and quiet and dedicated readers. Those able to read well became deeply involved and obviously benefited from the occasions. On the early occasions two children were in difficulties. One girl could not sustain a twenty-minute session and one boy regularly chose books he could not successfully read. Both soon adapted to the situation and have learned how to handle the period. [Howard Biggs of Childrey Primary School, Oxfordshire]

If I were asked to name the indispensable features of the reading environment – the provisions we cannot do without if we are to enable young people to become readers – Reading Time would be one of the essential four. Two others are a well-chosen book stock and reading aloud. The fourth comes under the heading 'Response' in the reading circle, and is the teacher-led talk that children do together about the books they've read. I deal with this aspect in Part Two: *Tell Me: Children, Reading and Talk*.

It is obvious that Reading Time ranks first of these four important features. For what is the use of providing a rich stock of books if none of them is ever read? And what is the point of talking about books which few in a group know well? And though reading aloud has value in itself, in the context of helping children become readers the question must be: How much do children read for themselves as a result?

Clearly, the provision of Reading Time gives purpose to all other reading-based activities. In fact, the quality of a school can be judged by its emphasis on providing time to read and by the strength of its determination to protect that time against all other demands.

8

Keeping Track

Forgetting is part of reading; remembering what we've forgotten is one of its pleasures.

We forget incidents, perhaps, or characters, or how the story goes. And few of us remember all the books we've ever read. For that reason, we reread the books we've enjoyed most. In rereading we recover what we enjoyed first time, and we discover details we hadn't noticed before which give us a deeper understanding, a changed view of the book.

Might it be that, if we kept a simple record of the books we read, we would increase our pleasure by making it easier to remember, as well as possible to remember more? Many great readers in the past have found it so. They accumulated their bibliography as they went along: title, author, date they finished reading. Some of them also kept notes on what they thought about the books.

During in-service courses I came across two teachers, both near retirement age, who had kept 'reading diaries' ever since they were teenagers. Each of them could open their notebooks at any page, point to an entry and immediately remember all kinds of things, not just about the book itself, but about where they were at the time, what they were doing, who they were with. Those of us who saw this happen envied them. A simple record had enriched their lives in a way the rest of us couldn't share. As a result I began keeping my own reading diary, and am very glad I did. Where reading is concerned, it's never too late.

But our reading history is much more than merely a list of books we happen to have read. It is intricately bound up with the story of how we came to think as we do, and how we came to be what we are – and what we wish we could be.

If reading doesn't affect our lives, doesn't change us or influence our behaviour, it is no more than a pass-time entertainment, and hardly worth all the fuss we make of it. But if reading affects our lives emotionally, intellectually, ethically, and in all sorts of other ways, as I believe it does, then it matters which books we put into our heads. And if it matters what we put into our heads, it also matters that we remember what those books were.

Besides, during school years, teachers have a public responsibility, placed on them by parents and the state, for what goes into children's heads. If a record of reading is not kept, how can teachers or anyone else discover a child's reading history? How can you deal intelligently with a class of children if you don't know which stories, poems, picture books and folk tales that group of children have experienced in the years before?

What used to happen when children learned to read by being drilled through the numbered sequence of books in a 'reading scheme' was that the teacher simply kept track of the numbers. Reading was a parade-ground skill. Nowadays the best teachers do for children what literary parents have always done. They surround their children with the best literature they can find and let them read what they like of it. These books aren't numbered. Nor are they sequenced in some drill-through order. Nor do all children read all the same books, whether in the same order or not.

These days, in any well-run classroom there will be some books that everyone has read and a great many that only some have read. There will also be books no one has read yet and others perhaps only one person ever will read. In any lively literate group everyone's reading history is unique but is based on a shared experience of certain books – those the community has somehow come to regard as essential.

Consequently, it is now necessary for children to keep their own reading diaries so that they and their parents and teachers can keep track. There is nothing onerous or difficult about this. It is another simple ritual that can be taught to children as soon as they are able to read and write, and something an adult can do for them until then.

It is equally necessary that children carry their diaries with them year to year, class to class, school to school. And in order to allow for the incompetent teacher or the one who refuses to accept the necessity or just doesn't bother, we should help children understand from the very beginning how valuable their diaries are and how important it is to keep them going no matter what their current teacher happens to think about it.

If we come across children who have never kept a diary, we should spend some time helping them catch up by recording as many books as they can remember from the missing period.

A FEW PRACTICAL POINTS

- Try to make sure reading diaries are kept in small bound notebooks. Pages are too easily lost from loose-leaf diaries. The notebooks don't need to be large or contain many pages, but they should be fairly stout so as to withstand childhood wear and tear.

- Before children can write for themselves, the teacher should make diary entries as the child watches, and keep the diaries safe between times. But as soon as children are able to write and are responsible enough to look after their diaries, they should do so, the teacher looking at them regularly while chatting about the books recorded.

- Don't insist that children write comments in their reading diary, which is simply a bibliographic record, not an exercise book. Some children like to write one-word judgements such as 'Great' or 'Boring' or 'Exciting', and there's nothing against this, but be wary of anything that turns diary-keeping into a chore.

- Avoid using the diaries as a means of assessment, such as teachers or parents writing judgemental comments against entries like 'This is too easy for you' or even 'Well done!', for this turns the diary into something other than an aid-to-memory, and, worse still, makes use of it against the child.

- Perhaps worst of all is when diaries are used to set one child against another in the name of competitive learning: 'Jennifer has read five books in the same time it has taken you, Sarah, to read only two, and you, Charles, have read none in the last two weeks, whereas James has read six.'

- If teachers are seen to keep their own reading diaries, children will keep theirs much more willingly.

9

STORYTELLING

Some people say they don't like reading stories, but I've never come across anyone who doesn't like hearing one.

Jokes, personal anecdotes, gossip (the story of our lives we tell each other in daily episodes), these are all narratives about people, telling what they did, how they did it, and why. This oral tradition goes back, the anthropologists tell us, to the earliest gatherings of human beings. And out of it have grown all the forms of literature – poetry, prose stories, drama – as well as history and biography, religion and philosophy: all the ways in which we use language imaginatively to tell each other about human life and try to make sense of it.

This is true of the history of the human race and it is also true of every individual human being. In this respect, each of us lives out the history of the race in the history of our own lives.

Everyone comes to printed literature through stories told aloud. Before we can speak, people play story-games with us. We call them nursery rhymes: *Hey diddle-diddle, the cat and the fiddle. Hickory-dickory-dock, the mouse ran up the clock. This little piggy went to market, this little piggy stayed at home.* And nursery tales: *Once upon a time there was a big bad wolf. Long, long ago there was a poor woman and her only son . . . And they all lived happily ever after.*

Simple words arranged in many story patterns – sounds that prepare us for what we may eventually meet in print. They accustom us to the music of language. They give us images to think, feel and perceive with. They store in our minds a cabinet of blueprints that help us recognize the architecture of narrative of different kinds and build stories of our own.

When we can talk, we are told stories that answer our questions about who we are and where we came from and why we are here. We hear stories about our family and stories about our tribe and stories about the world. And through these we place ourselves in time and space, and slowly construct identities that we call by our names.

If you doubt this, try playing a quite simple game with an acquaintance – someone you don't know too well. Ask each other: 'Who are you?', and question each other as you answer. Particularly ask the question: 'How do you know that?' You will perhaps be surprised by how difficult it is to explain who you are without telling a number of anecdotes – fragments of stories – and how often, when asked 'How do you know that?', you have to reply that someone told you so – your parents or grandparents or friends or neighbours. Indeed, if you play the game long enough, you may begin to wonder if you are only the stories you tell about yourself. Change the stories and you change your self!

Our taste for reading literature is deeply rooted in this oral experience of story, our need for it, and our understanding of its ways and means. Nursery rhymes and tales, the traditional folk and fairy stories – including fables, myths and legends – and the jokes and fantasies children pass on to each other: all these help form us as readers.

As I've said, it's not only young children who enjoy hearing stories; so do older children and adults. Think of that most successful form of popular entertainment, the soap opera. What is it but a televised form of fictional gossip? Think of how, when we visit friends, they like to show us the area where they live and tell us the stories associated with this building and that street, this field and that river, this person and that family. Think of the way we frequently explain everyday life to ourselves in the language of folk tales: of Cinderella, and the tortoise and the hare, and Beauty and the Beast, and the goose that laid the golden egg, and Robert the Bruce learning from the spider. Think of the fictional characters who inhabit our world as if they were as real as we are: Robin Hood, Father Christmas, Cinderella, Snow White. Think of why we persist, against the evidence, in regarding pigs as greedy, foxes as cunning, bears as cuddly friends, and sheep as stupid. And think of why it is so frequently reported that people who gave up reading fiction in their early teens take it up again when they become parents and, almost as if by instinct, begin telling their children the traditional rhymes and tales.

Storytelling is indispensable in enabling people to become literary readers, no matter what their age. In fact, there is evidence to suggest that unwilling teenage readers need to hear the old stories quite as much as do learner-readers of five and six, almost as a way of topping up on what they have missed before going any further as readers. Even more, they need to tell their own stories: the stories of their lives and the stories they've invented. For then they recover what they've forgotten or acquire something they were never given – a feeling for story we all need if we are to be self-sustaining readers who know how to play the reader's part in making sense of literature.

There are values storytelling shares with reading aloud, and I'll deal with those all together in the next chapter. Before that, some practical points.

1. STORYTELLING BEGINS WITH YOURSELF

Every adult has a collection of favourite yarns based on personal experience. Sharing these with children is an excellent way of establishing a good relationship with them, and then they in their turn will want to share something of themselves. And by showing not just a willingness but a desire to hear their stories, the adult confirms that the children's own-life stories matter, that they are as important, as interesting, as valuable as the stories made up by 'authors' (the invisible people who are the professionals).

Equally important are children's own made-up stories, and they have an added quality. Life stories provide their own logic: they actually took place in a sequence of events patterned by the chronology of clock time. Made-up stories, even when they use the raw material of lived experience, present narrative problems. Characters and incidents have to be invented, the plot has to be organized, the teller has to decide between past or present tense, third-person or first-person narrative, whether the narrator is an actor in the story or an observer of it, the balance of dialogue as against reportage, and so on.

By becoming authors in this way children draw on their experience of story in order to solve the problem of 'how to tell it'. And this practising of the art raises their level of interest in how others do it, with the result that they view story differently and they read differently – with a more conscious interest in form as well as content. They also begin to realize that readers aren't passive receivers but are active co-makers of stories who must 'fill the tell-tale gaps' – the indeterminacies – left by the author.

Here are some examples of indeterminacies in well-known picture books:

- In Maurice Sendak's *Where the Wild Things Are*, the reader must decide where the wild things are: in Max's head while he fantasizes, or in some place 'out there' to which he goes? If you prefer the first interpretation you'll find *Where the Wild Things Are* is a quite different story from the one experienced by a reader who prefers the second.

- In Anthony Browne's *A Walk in the Park* the reader must decide what all the incongruous items scattered through the book are doing there – Mickey Mouse looking over a wall, Father Christmas kicking a large red ball, Charlie Chaplin on the fountain, for example. What you decide will determine your understanding of the book.

- In John Burningham's *Granpa* the reader must piece together the dialogue without the help of any narrative commentary, and must decide what the empty chair at the end of the book means.

Only when we fill those gaps, and the many others like them to be found in every story no matter how simple it may seem, do we reach an understanding of what is being said and achieve a feeling of pleasure and satisfaction.

Children can do all this, learn all this, from listening to stories and telling their own, many months before they can read or write. Indeed, research suggests that a child's facility and progress as a reader of print depends on the richness of this preparatory storying.

2. BUILD YOUR OWN COLLECTION OF FAVOURITE STORIES FROM WRITTEN SOURCES

These will be of two main kinds:

- stories on which you can improvise, and
- stories that should be told exactly as they are written.

An example of the first kind is 'Cinderella'. Certain key incidents must be included, but there is no definitive way of telling them. The telling can be short or long, comic or romantic, naturalistic or satiric of social attitudes, and so on. Many folk and fairy tales are like that: plot structures on which the storyteller may embroider. Some invite improvisation but contain a few traditionally hallowed passages without which the tale doesn't seem to be quite right, such as the one in 'The Three Little Pigs' where the wolf says 'I'll huff and I'll puff and I'll blow your house down'.

Other stories are told with such personality of style that to tell them any other way is to remove their most essential quality. Beatrix Potter's Peter Rabbit stories and Rudyard Kipling's *Just So Stories* are like that. If we don't want to read these aloud, the only way to 'tell' them is to learn them by heart and repeat them exactly, like a pianist playing a score. What is left to the storyteller is the pacing of the tale, the treatment of dialogue and so on – the interpretation of the score, as it were. But then, this is also true of reading aloud. The difference is that when a story is told, the personality of the 'performer' makes a stronger direct impact on the audience than it does (or should) when the story is read aloud. The two activities are not the same. Storytelling is a performer-and-audience-focused activity; reading aloud is a text-focused activity. The shift from one to the other is important and changes the nature of the listener's experience.

3. CHOOSE CAREFULLY: NOT ALL STORIES SUIT ALL STORYTELLERS

Some people can be naturally funny, others cannot. Some people are good at 'doing the police in many voices', some are comfortable only with their own voice and yet can somehow make all the characters sound different. Some people like dramatizing a tale, making it theatrical (so they are hopeless with quiet, subtly understated stories), some like the conversational fireside style (so they are hopeless at very formal stories that must be told in a 'high' style).

Just as it would be tedious if we had to watch the same actor attempting every role no matter how inappropriate to his nature, so it is equally tedious for children to have to listen to one storyteller for, say, a whole school year. We should make sure that children hear stories told and read by a number of different people. This is another reason why teachers in a school should swap classes and groups frequently for storytelling and read-aloud sessions.

4. CHOOSE CAREFULLY: NOT ALL STORIES SUIT ALL AUDIENCES

But how do you know which stories to tell? The answer is simple: by trial and error. Though, as with all crafts, it is worth asking the advice of experienced practitioners.

If you're taking on a strange group, find out before you get there, or start by asking which stories they have been told in the last few days (infants), weeks (early juniors of six to eight), months (ages above eight). Then ask which are their favourites. This is useful in two ways.

First, if one of the favourites is in your collection it does no harm to begin by telling it again.

Second, we enjoy most that which is familiar enough for us to feel comfortable and yet is unfamiliar enough to excite us with its strangeness – the suspense of surprise. Knowing the stories that are familiar to an audience helps in selecting a new story similar to those already known yet sufficiently strange to create fresh interest.

At the start of a session give the audience time to get used to you with some very short stories that also prepare them for the direction you're going to take. Then when they are warmed up, move on to the main item on the bill. The pattern might be expressed thus: 'Hello, how are you today? . . . Try this for size . . . Ah, you like that, do you? Good . . . Now I've got you, here we go.'

5. BE PREPARED

Storytelling relies on improvisation and thinking on your feet, but that doesn't mean you don't need to prepare. The performers who look the most relaxed and spontaneous are usually the ones who have prepared and rehearsed the most carefully. Confidence (on which all successful 'spontaneous' performance depends) comes from knowing your material so well that you feel secure.

Everyone develops a special way of preparing but we all need to start somewhere. Here is Frances Clarke Sayers, a famous American storyteller, giving advice on how to set about it:

> After you have chosen a story you long to tell, read it over and over and over, and then analyse it. What in it has appealed to you? The humour? The ingenuity of the plot? What is its mood? And when you have isolated mood and appeal, consciously, this too will colour the telling of the story.
>
> Where is the climax? Make note of it in your mind, so that you can indicate to the children by pause, by quickening of the pace, the peak of the tale. Then read it again, and over and over. Then see if you can list, or call over in your mind, the order of the events of the story, the hinges of action, in their correct sequence. With these fully in mind, read the tale again, this time for turns of phrase you may want to remember. When these have been incorporated into your story, tell it to yourself, silently, just before you go to sleep at night, or while riding a bus or subway. After all this, you will find that the story is yours forever. For though you may forget it, after years of neglect, one reading of it will restore it to you, once you have mastered it thoroughly.

10

Reading Aloud

We cannot easily read for ourselves what we haven't heard said.

We learn to read by joining in with those who know how to do it, and gradually taking on all of the reading for ourselves. This 'loaning of consciousness' by the teacher to the learner constitutes what Lev Vygotsky calls the ZPD: 'the zone of proximal development'. Another way of putting it is to say that the learning reader becomes an apprentice.

Liz Waterland, a teacher of five- to seven-year-olds, thinks of reading like that. In *Read with Me* she describes how it works in practice:

> The adult first reads all the story while the child cannot read any, then the child will put in the words he or she knows while the adult reads the rest, then the child will take over the reading. All this with a known text, first of all, rather as the child learnt to speak a little at a time in forms that were familiar, until finally enough vocabulary is acquired to tackle new text (although still with an adult to help if needed). This, of course, at once negates the idea of books being 'too hard' for a child or the need for any form of colour coding, since the child can behave like a reader whatever the difficulty of the text and the adult will take over whatever the child cannot manage. We do not tell toddlers 'You may not try to say a word of three syllables until you can say all the words with only two.' When a child tries to say 'vegetable' we praise, not prevent – even if the word becomes 'vekble'.

The question being answered here is: What does the teacher do?

Enabling learner-readers turns out to be no different from what the skilled teacher does in every other learning activity. Jerome Bruner, an educational psychologist, summarizes it in these words:

> To begin with it was she [the teacher] who controlled the focus of attention. It was she who, by slow and often dramatized presentation, demonstrated the task to be possible. She was the one with a monopoly on foresight. She kept the segments of the task on which the child worked to a size and complexity appropriate to the child's powers. She set things up in such a way that the child could recognize a solution and perform it later even though the child could neither do it on his own nor follow the solution when it was simply told to him. In this respect, she made capital out of the 'zone' that exists between what people can recognize or comprehend when present before them, and what they can generate on their own – and that is the Zone of Proximal Development, or the ZPD. In general, what the tutor did was what the child could not do. For the rest, she made things such that the child could do with her what he plainly could not do without her. And as the tutoring proceeded, the child took over from her parts of the task that he was not able to do at first, but, with mastery, became consciously able to do under his own control. And she gladly handed those over.

Reading aloud to children is essential in helping them become readers. And it is a mistake to suppose that reading aloud is only needed in the early stages (the period people tend to call 'learning to read'). In fact it has such value, and learning to read is such a long-term process, and the bit we call 'learning' such a small part of it, that *reading aloud is necessary all through the school years.*

Ideally, every child should hear a piece of literature read aloud every day. Certainly, no teacher should be regarded as competent who does not ensure that this happens with the children in her charge. She may not read aloud to them herself every day, but she makes sure that someone does.

Recent accounts of developments in neuroscience – surveyed in the next chapter – can give us a glimpse of what happens in the brain when we are reading. They confirm what experience has always shown, that reading aloud is important for these reasons at least.

1. LEARNING HOW IT GOES

Every time we hear a story or a poem or any other kind of writing read aloud, we acquire another example of how that kind of writing 'works', how it is constructed, what to expect of it, and so on. In other words, listening to books read aloud prepares us for what we may find, and what we should look out for, as we perform the more difficult task of reading print for ourselves.

In listening to someone reading aloud, we place the burden of responsibility on her. We don't feel we must succeed with the print but that she must succeed in holding our attention. So we relax, we don't feel threatened, we're protected by the competence of the performer.

And as we listen we become used to the Text – not the print itself (which is usually called the text), but the experience of the story or poem as we know it inside our heads (which I've called the Text). When the time comes to tackle print on our own, we're prepared for what we find communicated by it. We know what kind of Text is held in the language of the text. (In fact we are finally able to tackle the text ourselves because we know what to expect it to do to us and what we must do to it.)

This is the process of 'taking it on' that Liz Waterland and Jerome Bruner describe. And it can't happen except through reading aloud.

Why? For this reason:

2. DISCOVERING THE DRAMA OF PRINT

How do we learn that the marks made on paper or on a screen are not just ways of representing words with dictionary meanings but are also capable of a kind of magic? If we know how, we can discover in them people who talk, events that happen, ideas we have never encountered before. They can frighten or amuse, can make us feel sad or happy, can invigorate and refresh us. No wonder non-readers find it hard to understand what it is that readers get from print, and how they get it, and sometimes think reading – or at least literary reading – is a mystery.

The only answer is that those who know how to work the magic show those who don't how it happens. The problem with print is that the results of bringing it alive take place inside the reader's head. They can't be taken out and displayed. The nearest we can come is to read aloud in such a way that listeners are given a sense of the drama we readers have found in a passage of print.

All writing is a kind of playscript. To enjoy a story or a poem you have to know how to convert print into the movement of action, the sound of characters thinking and talking, while giving every 'scene', every sequence, the right pace (slow or fast or a silent pause) that will turn printed information into vivid drama.

We discover how to do this when listening to someone bringing print alive by reading aloud, as we observe how the signals of punctuation and the rhythm of sentence structures are used to move the story along.

This means that learning listeners often need a copy of the text in front of them while they listen. Sometimes they prefer to listen first and go to the text afterwards to read it for themselves. What perhaps happens then is that they replay in their heads the memory of what they heard, and so in this way form their understanding of what successful readers do. This is one reason why so often, after hearing a story they've liked, children ask for a copy to look at.

One further point. As we listen to people reading aloud, we learn about interpretation. Different readings-aloud of the same text show clearly that what readers do is interpret. This is why repeated readings of a text are both useful and enjoyable. It is most easily done with poetry because poems tend to be short and can be repeated, differently interpreted, three or four times in one session. Indeed, it is a mark of the best literary writing in prose as well as poetry that we need to reread it before we can get the most out of it – the most understanding and the most pleasure.

Picture books are invaluable in this connection, because every picture book is in itself an interpretation of a text. The pictures not only add to the words in completing the whole story, but they are also a visual interpretation of the Text the artist 'saw' in his head. This is why the picture book is the natural form of literature for beginning readers, whatever their age: the theatre of the imagination in book form, showing us how readers' minds work as they read. Graphic novels are a good example of this form at its most complicated and adult.

3. 'DIFFICULTY'

At every age, whether child or adult, we are able to listen with pleasure and understanding to language that is too difficult for us to manage in print by ourselves. Reading development, like all human development, happens only if we knowingly reach out for something not quite in our grasp. Hearing what we cannot yet read for ourselves introduces us to texts we may decide we want to reach for.

Quite as importantly, listening to stories puts in our possession texts we might never attain in any other way. Within our community, we are more equal as listeners than we can ever be as readers. One of the things a teacher does is to make the experience of the 'too difficult' available by loaning her consciousness (see pages 50 and 51) as a reader-aloud of texts which the learners cannot yet, or may never, make their own in any other way. This in itself makes reading aloud essential.

4. STIMULATING CHOICE

Those who have tried it know that one of the best ways of encouraging children to read books they might otherwise ignore is to read extracts, or even the whole book, aloud.

Here are a few ways of arranging these occasions:

- A complete story is read at one sitting. Afterwards, nothing may be said, or a discussion may occur spontaneously, or there may be more formal talk led by the teacher (see Part Two, *Tell Me*). Some stories seem to provoke the need to talk about them, some have the opposite effect. The teacher will be sensitive to this and to what the children need. The main thing is that the story be experienced and enjoyed.

- A short programme of stories, poems, prose passages is compiled and read as a spoken anthology, either by one reader or by a group of readers. Between each piece there may be a brief interlude or a linking commentary or whatever else seems appropriate. This is an ideal form for open days, parents' evenings, school gatherings and other special occasions, when groups of children can give a prepared reading performance as an entertainment.

  An example: a class of ten-year-olds became interested in the poetry of Charles Causley, who they agreed was a very autobiographical writer. They decided to prepare a programme about him for their school's morning assembly. They selected ten of his poems, each of which spoke about a significant time in his life – his childhood in 'By St Thomas Water' and 'My Mother Saw a Dancing Bear', 'Convoy' for his time in the Royal Navy during the Second World War, 'Timothy Winters' for his work as a teacher, 'I Saw a Jolly Hunter' to represent his sense of humour, 'Mary Mary Magdalene' to communicate his love of his home town of Launceston in Cornwall as well as his strong sense of religion and mystery. And so on. The poems were linked with a narrative about Causley's life and character. The script – poems and commentary – was made into a book (they used a photograph album), illustrated with drawings to accompany the poems. After the performance the book was placed in the school library where it was greatly enjoyed. The assembly performance and the resulting book led many other children in the school to read Causley's poems for themselves.

- Part of a novel or long text is read in order to whet the appetite. The part chosen should have a unity of its own, so that hearing it is a satisfaction in itself, while not giving away the book's best surprises.

- A story is serialized over a few days. Ideally, there shouldn't be too long a gap between episodes. Some books lend themselves better than others to this kind of treatment.

- Short poems can be said at all sorts of times, in the breaks between work on one project and another, for example. But there should be times set aside specially for listening to poetry, even if just five or ten minutes in a day.

  I know teachers who have established a routine during the day for any child to put her name down to read a poem at the end of the afternoon just before everyone goes home. These children find a few minutes to rehearse their reading to avoid spoiling the poem or embarrassing themselves by fluffing it. When the time comes, each child in turn reads her chosen poem so that the school day ends with a kind of celebration, an anthology of verse to enjoy. It takes no more than ten minutes and is an admirable practice.

- Dramatized readings. A group of people – adults or children or a mix of both – prepare a text for speaking by a number of voices, rehearse it together, and then 'perform' it, perhaps with a minimal use of costumes and props, sound effects and music to add a theatrical touch – a hat, a cloak, a suitable dress, a frying pan: whatever is appropriate to the story that helps make a strong point. Usually when dramatizing stories in this basic way, the scriptwriter will include a narrator and divide the various characters' dialogue among members of the group, some of them doubling parts if necessary. Of course, all this can be elaborated into a full-scale play.

5. BEING TOGETHER

One of the most obvious and most notable aspects of reading aloud is its socially binding effect. Those who read together feel they belong together as a community, for nothing unites more than the sharing of their imaginary experiences; and they feel together physically, for reading aloud is essentially a domestic, a family-sized activity.

Everyone who has read to young children knows this is true. Children sit close, often hugged to you. They relax and become absorbed. As they listen they enjoy the security of belonging. Afterwards they use words, phrases, ideas, characters from the story in their own conversation – linguistic reference points, personal signposts that, for those who shared the experience, say much more than others can know.

This is how cultural identity is made. Of course storytelling and reading aloud both play a part, but each does it in different ways.

6. STORYTELLING AND READING ALOUD: THE DIFFERENCES

Storytelling is much more a relationship of teller speaking to listener. It is more like conversation, and feels personal, as if the storyteller is giving the listener something of himself.

In reading aloud the book literally objectifies the experience. Now the relationship is more like two people sharing something other than themselves. Not listener and teller looking at each other, but reader and listener, side by side, looking together at something else.

In reading aloud, the communication is always through words and pictures in print, coming from the unseen, usually unknown person of the author. This author, this person who is not present, has something to give us. It just happens that one of us is the reader. But all of us, including the reader, are receivers of the gift of the author's story.

Storytelling tends towards the emotionally dramatic; reading aloud tends towards the thoughtfully contemplative.

Storytelling tends towards the pleasure of an entertaining diversion; reading aloud tends towards the pleasure of self-recognition.

Storytelling tends towards the hermetic, the cabal, the exclusive group, limited to the powers of those who sit together. Reading aloud tends towards the permeant, the outward-looking, the inclusive group, whose powers are expanded by the addition of those in the text – powers of language, of thought, of the other, the author, who is not there.

Storytelling is culturally confirmative; reading aloud is culturally generative.

These distinctions require another book to examine. They are noted here as points for discussion.

IN PRACTICE

Time to Hear

If storytelling demands more from the performer, reading aloud demands more from the listener.

To begin with, reading aloud is less of a conversational art, less of a direct communication between teller and listener. In written language, meaning is usually more compacted, sentences are more densely constructed than in speech.

Second, quite often words in print depend on being seen if the reader is to catch their double meanings. Sometimes the way they are set out on the page is important to their understanding. In storytelling, the performer can explain and repeat and cut and edit as he goes along, and make all this seem part of the story. The reader-aloud can't be quite so adaptable to the audience. He has an authorized text to follow: Explaining and changing as he goes along may ruin it. Thus the listener needs more time to take in the meaning and to understand what is happening. So reading aloud usually has to be slower in delivery than storytelling.

Time to Look

Because the source of reading aloud is a visible text, learning readers (of all ages, but young children especially) often like to look at the book as well as at the reader while they listen. And often when a story has been enjoyed they want to hear it again, or read it for themselves. When planning a reading you should take these impulses into account. How can the text be shown to listeners if they want to see it? Will copies be available if they want to read it afterwards?

Time to Prepare

Never read a story to children until you've read it yourself. Why? First, if you don't know what's coming next, you might easily find yourself reading out something embarrassing or unsuitable. Second, very few people are so good at sight-reading that they can afford to be unprepared, which means more than simply reading the text silently beforehand. Language that you can 'hear' quite easily in your head can turn out to be very tricky indeed to read aloud. So read aloud to yourself before reading to others.

Of course, careful selection of texts appropriate to your audience is essential. If you select and prepare well, you can afford to relax during the performance, giving yourself up to the words, enjoying them as much as you hope the audience will. And then you can allow the session to shape itself, because whatever happens you'll feel secure with the 'script'. Whether to speak or listen, allow interruptions or not, pause or go on, break off sooner than intended or continue longer – these things will sort themselves out according to the mood of the audience and the needs of the moment.

'All of this,' wrote Frances Clarke Sayers in words endorsed by people with long experience of reading aloud, 'demands a great investment of time. Yet there is hardly any other investment, hardly any other area of study, that yields so potent a means of making literature live for children.'

11

Reading and the Brain

Scientists who study the brain now have considerable evidence of what happens in the brain when we read. What they are discovering informs what we should do to help people become competent readers. The scientific evidence is available in an increasing number of internet websites, magazine articles and books. What we're finding out is of such importance that I've tried to summarize the essential features. But this is only a beginning.

Some basic statements:

- We are not genetically engineered to be readers. Reading and writing are inventions of the human race. It has taken many thousands of years to develop our brains for this purpose. It is true that the brain of every individual has to live that history.
- The human brain has infinitely more capacity – is bigger – than we can imagine. It is not a computer. It is more like a self-organizing system. It is also self-teaching. It changes with use throughout our lifetime. Mental concentration alters the physical structure of the brain.
- Reading is one of the most complicated processes our brains perform.
- When we are reading silently three parts of the brain, at least, are being used:
- One part processes the sounds associated with the words, pictures, etc.

- One part processes the visual information – the letters, words, pictures, etc.
- One part processes the meaning of the words, sentences, and the whole text, relating this new text to what it already knows. It seems that we have an archive in the brain, which stores everything we have ever heard said, or have read. When faced with a new text, the brain searches through its archive to find anything that 'matches' with something in the new text. If no match can be found, we say the text is too difficult for us. The more matches the brain finds the easier it becomes for us to read the new text.

Here is how Sebastian Wren, a specialist in the reading process, expresses it:

> Right now, as you are reading this passage of text, your occipital cortex is very active, processing all the visual information you are encountering – the words, the letters, and the features of the letters. The frontal lobe of your neocortex is engaged in processing the meaning of the text you are reading – meanings of the words, sentences, and the big picture, and it is working to relate what you are reading with what you already know. Surprisingly, your temporal lobe (particularly on the left side of your brain if you're right handed) is also active now, processing all the 'sounds' associated with reading – even though you're already reading silently to yourself, the areas of the brain that process speech sounds are active just like they would be if you were listening to somebody speak. Your brain is very structured in the way it processes information. Complex tasks such as reading a passage of text are broken down into easier tasks, and the easier tasks are distributed to the areas of the brain that specialize in those tasks.

Wren ends with a warning:

> Neuroscience is a relatively new field, and the best researchers in the field do not know much more about the operations of

> the brain during reading than what has been described in this short article. It has been said that we know considerably less about the workings of the human brain than we know about distant stars and galaxies in our universe. We are learning a great deal, but there is a great deal more to be learned. For now, it is most prudent to adopt a healthy scepticism about claims made about 'brain based' reading programs.
>
> [Pulled from the internet, 07/03/2009.
> http://www.sedl.org/reading/topics/brainreading.html]

With that health warning in mind, there are two points that can be safely made:

- Reading aloud is essential to reading development even when the learner is able to read silently to themselves, because the area of the brain that deals with sound has to function as competently as the other two areas and it can only do so if it is familiarized with the sound of new words, sentences, and texts. That's why it's always easier to read silently to yourself a text you have first heard read aloud.
- Because all reading is dependent on what has already been read, the greater the variety of words, sentences and texts the brain has in its archive the better able it is to make sense of new texts. The more references you have stored in your memory bank the richer you are and the better you can read.

As Maryanne Wolf, herself a neuroscientist and a specialist in dyslexia, says in *Proust and the Squid: The Story and Science of the Reading Brain*, one of the most helpful books on the subject I've come across:

> If there are no genes specific only to reading, and if our brain has to connect older structures for vision and language to learn this new skill, every child in every generation has to do a lot of work. As the cognitive scientist Steven Pinker eloquently remarked, 'Children are wired for sound, but print is an optional accessory that must be painstakingly bolted on.' To acquire this unnatural process, children need instructional

environments that support all the circuit parts that need bolting for the brain to read.

Wolf mentions three studies which provide stark evidence of the deprivation caused by impoverished environments. The first was

> a chilling finding in a study of one California community by Todd Risley and Betty Hart [which] exposes a bleak reality with serious implications: by five years of age, some children from impoverished-language environments have heard 32 million fewer words spoken to them than the average middle-class child. What Lousia Cook Moats calls 'word poverty' extends well beyond what the child hears. In another study, which looked at how many words children produce at age three, children from impoverished environments used less than half of the number of words already spoken by their more advantaged peers.

What goes in is what comes out.

Wolf then turns her attention to the availability of books.

> In a survey of three communities in Los Angeles, there were startling differences in how many books were available to children. In the most underprivileged community, no children's books were found in the homes; in the low-income to middle-income community there were, on average, three books; and in the affluent community there were around 200 books. [...] The sheer unavailability of books will have a crushing effect on the word knowledge and world knowledge that should be learned in these early years.

Next Wolf mentions another of the factors that enrich the environment and the development of the reading brain.

> In a broad study of early development of literacy skills, the educator Catherine Snow of Harvard and her colleagues found that in addition to literacy materials, one of the major

contributors to later reading was simply the amount of time for 'talk around dinner.' The importance of simply being talked to, read to, and listened to is what much of early language development is about, but the reality in many families (some economically disadvantaged, some not) means that too little time will be given to even these three basic elements before a child reaches the age of five.

Wolf is talking about the early years. The fact is these three elements matter all through a child's educational life: hearing a wide range of language and language use; books and texts of all kinds being available; and talk in which the child is listened to as well as spoken to. This last element is the topic of Part Two: *Tell Me*.

In sum, what we now know for certain is that hearing texts read aloud, having a wide range of texts available, and being engaged in talk about what we've read are not optional extras in education, they are not theoretic ideology, nor is the argument based only on anecdotal evidence. We can show by reference to scientific investigation that they are essential to the wise and proper education of all readers.

12

Star Performers

Meeting authors and illustrators bridges the gap between children and books in a way that no other experience can.

A little girl once asked me, 'Do real people write books?' Finding the answer to that question is perhaps the main reason most people, not only children, enjoy meeting the individuals who make the books they like to read. Cold print takes on a human face. Certainly all the evidence we have – in what children tell us after the event, in increased sales and borrowings, in the writing children do for themselves, in what the publishers report – suggests that authors and illustrators are the star performers among those who enable children to become readers.

Not that the benefits are all one way. Writers and illustrators get plenty in return. They learn from their audience, who help them keep in touch with real readers. They are made to justify their work, children being uninhibited inquirers into every detail of it. And they have some fun – a day or two of relief from what can be a lonely job.

Many schools arrange visits from writers and illustrators two or three times a year, and other special guests too, for it isn't only the originators who can play this role. Translators, publishers, printers, booksellers, librarians, professional storytellers help children discover the variety of skills that go into making books and the variety of ways we can enjoy them.

But there are practical problems that need attention.

CHOOSING THE PERFORMER

Sometimes making a choice is easy. For example, when there is a well-known local writer, or when the district librarian offers an illustrator who is touring the area. Then the visitor is personally known beforehand to someone (yourself, the district librarian) who can assess whether he will be successful with children. Just because a writer's books are popular or critically much admired doesn't mean he is a successful performer. So before inviting someone unknown, it's best to find out tactfully what he's like in person and in public.

MAKING THE APPROACH

If you don't know a private address, make your approach to an author or illustrator via the publicity department of her/his publisher. This can often be done by email. If by post, include a stamped, self-addressed envelope. And include the following details:

- Your school's name, address, telephone number, email address.
- A brief outline of the reason for the invitation and what you hope the guest will do.
- The kind of event you have in mind and whether other guests will be appearing.
- The age and numbers of the children involved.
- Whether the guest's books will be on sale or not.
- A selection of suitable dates in the hope that one of them will be convenient for the guest.
- The fee and expenses you can offer.
- The accommodation you can offer, should the visit require an overnight stay. (Not everyone, by the way, enjoys being the houseguest of a family, however much the family might like it. But if you can't afford a hotel, say so.)

In subsequent correspondence, if not in this first contact, you'll want to establish:

- The number and length of the sessions.
- The kind of session the guest will offer: give a talk to a small or large group, run a workshop, meet staff and parents, etc.

- Any special requirements of the guest.
- Whether there will be a book-signing session.
- What equipment might be needed: audio-visual aids, Powerpoint, display boards, tables, large drawing board, etc.
- Whether helpers are needed.
- Which books the guest might especially talk about (so that you can obtain copies beforehand and prepare the children if necessary).
- How the guest will reach the venue: clear printed directions, for arrival by car; arrangements to meet arrival by public transport.

The more efficient and businesslike you can be, the more likely you are to receive a favourable reply and to avoid calamities on the day.

And it goes without saying that visits should usually be arranged at least three months ahead. Indeed, the most successful star performers tend to be booked up at least a year in advance.

ON THE DAY

- Make sure that someone is responsible for greeting guests on arrival, seeing to their needs, and generally making them comfortable.
- Make sure any equipment being used actually works, can easily be replaced if it goes wrong, and that it is handled by someone competent.
- If there are to be formal introductions and votes of thanks, see that what is said about the guest is accurate and brief.
- Make sure everyone in the school knows of any changes to the usual routine of the day and see that the guest's sessions won't be interrupted.
- Be sensitive to a guest's needs. Sometimes in the excitement, organizers forget that guests might like a few minutes' rest between sessions, or some refreshment, or even that they need to go to the lavatory. At other times organizers can be so protective that a guest is whisked away at the end of every session and hidden in an empty room when he might actually prefer to spend some time informally with the children or the staff.

MAKING THE MOST OF A VISIT

A star performer's visit ought to be the climax to a great deal of reading-based preparation, and even more reading activity should result from it.

Beforehand, children will be involved in making arrangements, in reading the visitor's books, in creating displays, in writing and illustrating their own stories for the visitor, in dramatizing scenes, in deciding on the questions they want to ask, and the like. The visit should be a stimulus, providing a real purpose and out-of-the-ordinary energy for exceptional work.

After it's over, the visit should be discussed: best moments retold, worst moments learned from for the next time. Requests for the visitor's books should be satisfied. A scrapbook of the visit might be made. Photographs and videos of the event can be shown. Successful classroom events prepared for the guest (dramatizations, for example) can be performed again for other classes or for parents, or even developed further. Anything learnt about writing or drawing or storytelling or printing – whatever insights the guest brought – should be exploited in children's own work of the same kinds. And don't forget to:

- Send the guest and any outside helpers a letter of thanks (something else children can help with).
- Make sure fees and expenses are paid promptly, if they cannot be paid on the day of the visit.
- Report on the event to those who can help the school again (Arts Council, school governors, head librarians, sponsors, PTA, the local newspaper).

From my own experience and from the experience of scores of teachers reported to me during in-service courses, I know that two conclusions about the visits of star performers are common: they are exhausting for the organizers (and usually everyone else as well, not least the guest), and they are immensely worthwhile and have long-lasting effects on children's reading lives.

It is equally true, however, that those benefits depend greatly on careful planning, attention to detail, and the organizers putting themselves out during the event.

13

Friends and Peers

Several years ago, after spending a great deal of money on research, the American Booksellers Association announced the not very surprising fact that far and away the commonest reason for choosing a book is that we have heard about it from our friends.

Though this information may not be of much use to commercial booksellers, it is of considerable use to the enabling adults who work with children. It tells us that time spent encouraging talk between children about books they've read pays off in helping them read more. And that if we can influence the reading of the leaders and opinion-makers among groups of children, they will pass on their enthusiasm to others.

A lot of this work is done informally, of course, when chatting with individual children out of class, and at times when we're teaching one-to-one. We mention a book and loan a copy 'specially for you'. We find out what a child is reading that we'd like others to know about and suggest she talk to this or that friend about it

This is improvisational teaching and its success depends on knowing the children very well and knowing the books just as well so that at the right moment we can suggest the right book to the right child.

There are also more formal teacherly techniques to help children share their reading and widen the spread of their influence on each other. Here are some of them:

'HAVE YOU READ THIS?' SESSIONS

These are times set aside for children to tell each other about books they have liked so much they want other people to read them too.

Sometimes, of course, this happens spontaneously. Sarah, for instance, mentions to her teacher that she has just finished a marvellous book; the teacher asks her there and then to tell the rest of the group about it.

Waiting on the moment isn't enough, however. Nor do such times give the child reviewer a chance to prepare. You need to build into the week's activities a set time when three or four pupils can present a book each. You should make sure they think about what they'll say beforehand, that they have a copy of their chosen book to show, and that they look for details that might help make their review more interesting – information about the author, for example, or about other similar books, or a picture of the setting.

Afterwards, the rest of the group should be encouraged to ask questions and to add their own comments, with the teacher acting as chairperson, making sure that everyone gets a chance to speak, and helping when necessary. Perhaps at the end the teacher can summarize the main things that were said, and finish by mentioning titles and authors again while showing the books in order to fix them in the children's memories. If possible, copies of the recommended books should be available for people to read.

It's easy to see how this basic plan can be varied and developed. Large groups can be split into smaller, each holding a 'Have you read this?' session of its own, then reporting back to the whole group at the end, the chosen books being displayed for a day or two. One class can do it for another, or older children for younger. I've come across schools who have paired with other schools to swap online, audio or video recordings of book-panel sessions prepared specially for their partners. Others have shared their reading at one of their PTA meetings and at morning assemblies.

Some teachers extend the idea to a written version. They keep a large-size card file or a loose-leaf 'Have you read this?' book. Now this is expanding into online exchanges. Pupils are encouraged to write about a book they've very much enjoyed, so that others looking for a book to read can share it. The recommendation may be as brief as a single comment, or it may take the form of a longer, more carefully considered review. (One memorable entry said simply 'This is a book Carole should read.')

As a secondary school boy once told me, 'When books are recommended by your own age group you tend to go for those rather than the ones a teacher has recommended.' Whether this is generally true I'm not sure. There are young readers who would say just the opposite. But with those for whom it is true, 'Have you read this?' sessions are the best method by which a teacher can put peer group influences to work.

BOOK GRAFITTI BOARDS

I came across this idea in a secondary school and have since seen it used very successfully in junior and infant schools as well. It comes from the pleasure people take in scrawling messages on walls.

All that's needed is a pin-up noticeboard in a classroom or corridor. The rule is simple. Anything can be stuck on it so long as the intention is to recommend a book. This means the title and author must be clearly legible.

What kind of item gets stuck up? I've seen:

- book covers made by readers
- blurbs copied from book covers and decorated long reviews written by readers
- verses about the book
- appropriate emblems (a large black spider with '*Charlotte's Web* by E. B. White' written on it)
- numerous parody letters suggested by *The Jolly Postman* by Janet and Allan Ahlberg
- photographs (cut from *Radio Times*, newspapers, old magazines) of authors, of settings, of anything connected to a book
- book publicity postcards, posters, stickers, badges
- extracts from a book produced on a computer and decorated
- child readers' own illustrations
- and, inevitably, jokes of all sorts based on books.

Once children understand the idea, their enthusiasm is such that the board is quickly filled. The problem is to let things stay up long enough to have an effect. One infant school solved this by having a graffiti scrapbook: as soon as the board was full, the children chose the most effective items from it and stuck them into a large scrapbook. The scrapbook was kept in their library so that anyone could look at it at any time.

MAGAZINES

They may be ephemeral, like wall newspapers, or more permanent, like the school magazine; they may be audiovisual (online 'book programmes', for example). Whatever the form, as with the graffiti board, the aim is to include book-related items that may attract readers to the books mentioned, anything from reviews to jokes.

SELECTION PANELS

Every chance should be taken of involving children in selecting books for class and school libraries and for displays and exhibitions.

Making decisions about selection requires discussion, sharing of opinions, thinking out the qualities and weaknesses of different kinds of book, and, of course, a lot of reading. If the panel members represent class groups they must canvass their peers for their views, and this involves further critical talk. The whole business has a real purpose (books are actually going to be read by others who will expect the choice to be justified) which gives it an importance lacking in mere classroom exercises.

All sorts of useful questions will have to be confronted: How do you judge a book? What are you looking for when selecting for other people as well as for yourself? What is a 'good' book? What kinds of words help you make your thoughts clear? Are there different ways of reading? And what are they? The questions may not be phrased in those words, but they will underlie a lot of the talk that goes on, and the teacher's job is sometimes to bring them to the surface in a way that the children can understand.

DISPLAYS

It is worth mentioning display-making again to remind us of the value of the activity in encouraging the people who do this and in influencing others in their choice of reading. (See Chapter 5.)

READING CLUBS

Like all fans and connoisseurs in any field, people who are especially keen readers sometimes like to gather together. It's important that avid readers feel supported and get a chance to do more with books than in-school time allows. Obviously, what can be done depends a lot on the age and circumstances of the children. But generally speaking, reading clubs provide occasions for storytelling and reading aloud, visits from interesting guests for talks about books of the kind that might not suit classroom groups, book-related film and online shows, discussions about how to improve the reading environment in the school and then putting ideas into action, and so on.

Reading clubs should help enthusiastic readers enjoy books even more, but they should also be bases from which a body of keen readers can influence the whole community.

PUPIL ORGANIZERS

When people, no matter what their age, are involved in the organization of an activity, they tend to become even more enthusiastic about it, and to influence the attitudes of others to it.

From playgroup to college, there are opportunities for all ages and abilities to help with the organization and provision of books – anything from playgroup kids helping to pack away their books from the book corner at the end of the morning to college students running their own bookshop. Assisting in the class and school library, making displays, ordering and buying stock, producing publicity for the bookshop, running a book magazine, being in charge of the graffiti board . . .

It's my experience, as I know it is other teachers', that once young people are working together as readers, the problem is not finding ways of bringing peer influence to bear but finding time and resources to satisfy the demands they make for more and more books and more and more time to read because of the enthusiasm they generate among themselves. Equally, I'm one of many who have observed the extraordinary effect on the reading life of a school as these peer group activities develop.

This way of working is a very good example of the kind of teaching that is not done directly, but that puts the teacher in the role of catalyst, someone who causes things to happen – the enabler who works through others: a facilitator, a provider of resources, a guide, an administrator, a background figure. In the end, what learners do for themselves, guided by a skilled teacher-provider, is more effective than anything teachers do for learners who are not involved in helping each other.

14

Helping to Choose

Selecting books to buy for children's collections, arranging displays, telling stories and reading aloud, encouraging children to talk to one another about the books they've read, inviting authors and illustrators to meet young readers: these are the important ways adults help children choose books to read, which is why I've given them chapters of their own.

But there are other ways that are worth mentioning.

BY-THE-WAY CONVERSATIONS

Much can be done informally, both inside the classroom and outside, in helping individual children choose a book. These are times when you can fit the choice most closely to the pupil and when you and the pupil can uninhibitedly share your reading – opinions and prejudices, tastes and pleasures. We listen best to other people's views when we know they respect ours. When an adult takes a genuine interest in a child's own choice of book, the child is likely to take up the adult's suggestions about what to try next.

This informal, friendly gossip about books is fundamental to our success in more formal dealings with groups of readers.

'TRY THESE'

(A version of 'Have you read this?', page 70.) Now and then devote a five-, ten-, twenty-minute session to talking about a few books you'd like the children to read. Tell a little of the plot, read a passage that might whet the appetite, explain what you like and what you think are some of the attractive qualities of each book. Tell anything enticing you know about the author, or the writing of the book, or any other detail that may help raise interest. Be careful not to say too much, and three books are the maximum, as a general rule.

MIX AND MATCH

Gather various versions of the same book – hardback, paperback, other-language, large print and braille editions, taped readings, film and TV dramatizations – for everyone to look at and compare covers, blurbs, illustrations, the effect of the different typographic designs, hearing the story as against reading it for yourself, the dramatized version as against the written, and so on. Even when readers claim not to like a story, exploring it in this way often overcomes their dislike and usually increases their interest in books generally and in what reading is, how we do it, and what it does to us.

In the same way, put together mini exhibitions of all (or most) of the books by an author you want the children to get to know, such as all the picture books of Shirley Hughes or all the books of Philip Pullman or all the poetry books compiled by Anne Harvey, along with related material and objects, and talk about them.

Or take three or four books retelling the same story, as in versions of folk and fairy tales, or various editions of the same fiction, like Rudyard Kipling's *Just So Stories*, each differently illustrated, and let children compare them, choosing the ones they prefer.

RAISING EXPECTATIONS

All this activity raises expectations of pleasures to come from reading. We need to be sure that these expectations can be fulfilled.

I once heard a teacher telling a class that they would like Lucy Boston's *The Children of Green Knowe* because it was such a good ghost story. In children's minds, ghost stories usually mean clanking chains, horrific spectres and spinechilling sensations. There is none of that in *The Children of Green Knowe*. It was predictable that most of the children would be disappointed, and the book would take the blame for not being something it was never intended to be.

Better to undersell than oversell! Express doubts, be tentative rather than assertive, warn about 'boring' passages or slow starts or difficult words here and there. But all the time let your own enjoyment show.

Make it quietly plain that you expect more of them as readers than the children themselves think they can manage. Help them to take pleasure in 'difficulty' – the book that is on the edge of their forward reach, the kind of story or poetry they haven't yet managed to appreciate, the writer they have never heard of before. After all, what are teachers for, if not to help us go where we cannot go on our own?

15

Response

Reading is a provocative act; it makes things happen.

Rereading. One of the most important results is wanting to read again: reread the book we've just finished, or read another. This, of course, is the 'response' teachers of reading are hoping for the most. They want to see their pupils starting around the reading circle again because they know that to become a literary reader you have to read continually.

Time to reflect. Readers frequently need time to digest a book they've just finished. They want to savour the pleasure, explore their understanding of what it has said to them, share their enjoyment and their understanding with others – usually, as we've seen, with their friends (who they hope will read that book too).

Reading is a social activity. It is at its most social when we share our reading by talking about it, in a kind of profoundly important gossip. Children should be encouraged in this, which means giving them time to chat informally together without teacherly impositions. And it means chatting with them ourselves so that they hear how we gossip – the language we use, the topics we talk about, the way we listen to others – and witness our enthusiasm for print.

But if we are to help children become thoughtful readers, informal gossip isn't enough. We must help them develop their inborn facility to question, report, compare, discriminate. Teaching of this kind is a specialist skill. You need to have studied it and thought it out, need to have become practised yourself at the kind of responsive talk which is more structured, more consciously organized, and goes deeper than everyday gossip.

So far this book has been devoted to the practical business of arranging a reading environment where responsive talk – what I call booktalk – can thrive. The skill of teaching responsive booktalk is discussed in Part Two, *Tell Me: Children, Reading and Talk*. What needs to be said here is that our talk about books, more than anything else, enlarges and deepens us as readers.

There are other helpful forms of response that children enjoy. Here is a checklist of some of them.

'FOR THE AUTHOR'

Children make a 'book about the book' and display it for others to see, or send it to the author as their part in the 'literary discourse'. It might contain their thoughts about what they liked and disliked or found puzzling. Pictures suggested by their reading are often included, as are some of the children's own stories and poems and other kinds of writing. When appropriate, jokes and cartoons are popular, of course, and sometimes photographs. Anything can be included that the children feel best expresses what they want to say to the author. Computer versions of this are now possible, with enormous potential still unexplored.

PAINTING AND ILLUSTRATING. MAKING MODELS

Many children find it easier, more pleasurable, and certainly less inhibiting to respond by making a picture or a model than by writing. I remember, for example, a class of children producing a sequence of pictures, one for each of the calamities in *The Eighteenth Emergency* by Betsy Byars. And I've lost count of the number of times I've seen enormous constructions of foil-covered cardboard boxes standing in primary school entrance halls as representations of the eponymous hero of Ted Hughes's everlastingly popular *The Iron Man*.

Some children, especially at the age of seven or thereabouts, talk more easily when they are using their hands and making things. The details we find in their paintings or models lead quite naturally to questions about the thinking behind them. This in turn draws them into talk about their reading and their understanding of the details they found in a book.

ANTHOLOGIES

Poetry is perhaps the hardest of all forms of writing to talk about. The most natural response is to ask to hear the poems read aloud again, or to copy out favourites to keep in a personal anthology. Some of the most successful and enjoyed approaches to poetry with children that I've come across have been achieved by teachers who encouraged children to keep their own personal and class anthologies. Every day some poems are read aloud to start the day or end it, or in breathing spaces between jobs. The most liked poems are copied into anthologies – handwritten, typed, wordprocessed, cut out and pasted down when that is practicable – sometimes decorated or illustrated.

ACTING IT OUT

It seems instinctive in younger children to respond to stories and poems by turning them into play, acting out scenes, or inventing new ones so that the story becomes their own. Older children love to formalize this in dramatized performances, whether improvised or scripted. Adaptations for puppets, 'radio' and video, the full-blown business of theatre, dramatized readings in which the text has been rewritten to suit a narrator and character voices: all these are frequently used. As an author I've sometimes been entertained by children who have adapted my books. As a teacher I know how much time and work this costs (much more than painting and model-making, for example). But I've always been moved, as well as amused, by the pleasure this kind of response gives children and the amount they can learn from it about the original text, themselves and each other.

BOOK MAKING

Becoming a writer and book producer is one of the best ways to explore the writing of other people. Children are nowadays widely encouraged to find out how a book as a physical object is made, what it is that professional writers say about writing, and to try to become both writers and book-makers themselves. And making books does satisfyingly complete the circle which began by selecting something to read. There is an intricate relationship between writing and reading, both as process and as ways into and out of a text. Both are creative, both are interpretive acts. What you discover by writing is not the same as what you discover by reading. By becoming both writer and reader you can possess it all.

16

Books in a Digital Age

When is a book not a book?

Which begs the question: What *is* a book?

These days you can obtain a book online and read the text on any one of many kinds of screen, including Portable Reader Systems, usually called eReaders for eBooks.

Does it matter how a book is delivered and on what device, paper or electronic, it is read?

Is the experience the same, whatever the form of delivery?

In this book I talk not just about reading, regardless of the kind of text, but about reading books. And though what I'm saying applies to the reading of all kinds of texts, however delivered, my particular interest is in the reading of the kinds of text we call literature. By which I mean, to use David Daiches's simple definition, 'any kind of composition which has for its purpose not the communication of fact but the telling of a story (either wholly invented or given a new life through invention) or the giving of pleasure through some use of the inventive imagination in the employment of words.'

Clearly such a definition encompasses not only stories and novels but poetry, what used to be called belles lettres, as well as some treatments of biography, history, religion, philosophy, science, and politics.

Which raises another question. When you're reading, say, a novel on a computer screen are you reading the same composition, to use Daiches's word, as you are when reading it in a traditional book?

I'll return to this after clearing up a prior question on which it depends. Because whether you are or not depends on what a book *is*.

Which means we need a definition.

Here is one I've tested with many people. (Let's remember that a definition must include only the elements necessary to the object in question, without qualifying conditionals.)

A book is
a sequence of pages
on which appear
meaning-communicating signs
all of which are bound together
in an authorized order.

Let's unpack what the definition implies for readers.

A BOOK IS

An obvious fact of a traditional book is that it is composed of a number of pages. A single page, a single leaf of paper printed on both sides, doesn't make a book. Nor do any number of loose pages, no matter how many. Necessarily, a book contains more than a few pages, and the pages must belong together in some kind of related sequence that makes a whole. So:

A BOOK IS A SEQUENCE OF PAGES

And of course books communicate something. A gathering of blank pages does not make a book, unless a conditional adjective is applied: a drawing book, a notebook, an account book. These are incipient books. They are waiting for someone to inscribe communicating signs on their blank surfaces. They are would-be but not-yet books.

As for the signs – letters, words, figures, diagrams, maps, musical notations, mathematical and scientific formulae, etc. – these can be inscribed onto blank pages in many ways: by hand with pencil, ink and brush, by traditional mechanical printing methods and nowadays by electronic devices. Nor need the pages be made of paper. There are synthetic materials capable of displaying electronically delivered signs, and yet the pages are presented as a book or as an eReader. So we cannot simply say that books are only those printed in long-familiar ways or written by hand as in the times before moveable type.

It doesn't matter how the signs get there so long as the means of delivery conforms to the other elements required by the definition.

ON WHICH APPEAR MEANING-COMMUNICATING SIGNS

It is no longer sufficient to say books are 'printed'. The signs appear on the pages by various means, and the signs themselves communicate meanings of various kinds. We read books because 'they make sense' not just of one kind but of many different kinds from novels to treatises, from poetry to maths.

ALL OF WHICH ARE BOUND TOGETHER

Books are made of pages bound together. Binding is not used simply to stop the pages being lost or shuffled into the wrong order. And it isn't only the pages that are bound together. The definition says 'all of which', meaning not only all the pages but the sequence of the pages and the signs that appear on the pages.

The whole thing – pages and signs – are bound together in order to preserve the book's integrity.

A book is bound because the binding maintains:

AN AUTHORIZED ORDER

This is the heart of the matter.

A book is more than simply a convenient and user-friendly form of presenting written language. It is a form of communication determined by the author of the text. It is the author who has decided on the signs that are written and the order in which the signs are arranged and the order, the sequence, of the pages on which the signs appear.

Fundamentally and essentially, a book is a book because it is authored. And because the ordering decided on by the author is sacrosanct. The order must not be interfered with and the signs must not be changed to suit the preferences of a reader or anyone else.

There is an authority involved in a book.

And a second authority comes into play once a book is made.

TWO KINDS OF AUTHORITY

The first is the primary authority of the author, who arranged the words on the page, arranged the pages in a sequence, and indicated her intention by binding it all together.

To interfere with this order, to rearrange or delete any of the words or pages, is a violation. A book requires those who use it to exercise particular responsibilities, one of which is to preserve the integrity of the author's composition, whatever the user might think about it.

The second authority is the co-equal authority of the user / reader. He may do as he pleases with the book itself, for who can prevent him? He can use it as a doorstop if he likes, and, if he owns the copy, he can tear pages out. If he reads it, he can read it backwards if he prefers, he can dip and delve, skip and reread. In this sense, the reader is in charge and the author is powerless.

But a responsible reader honours an unwritten contract to respect what the author has made and not tamper with it. He will sample the text in order to decide whether it is something he wants to give his time and energy to read. But when he decides the text is worthwhile, he honours what the author has made by attending to it *as a whole and in the bound-together sequence*.

Looked at from the readers' point of view, authors have a responsibility to them, just as readers have a responsibility to the author. Authors must respect readers by giving the best of themselves to their work – the totality of their skill, knowledge, experience, understanding, care, and above all, their command of language.

This mutual respect and bipartite authority are sited not in the author and the reader as persons, but in the Book. The Book is the source of their pleasure. It is the Book, the making of it and the reading of it, which creates their authority. The Book is the location and the focus of their respect and attention. It is the Book that authorizes them.

Responsible authors and readers know this. They talk of how a particular book absorbs them, of how they can lose themselves in it, of how it takes them over, lives in them, changes them, however minutely, each time, how it adds to their experience, knowledge, development, personality. They value most those books that transcend their individual ability to use language, present ideas, inquire into human behaviour. The books that matter most to authors and readers are those that speak to them and speak for them, expressing better than they can themselves that which they already know and that which they are glad to learn.

THE BOOK AND OTHER MEDIA

All of which may be the case, but is it any the less so of, say, film or a stage play or a TV or radio programme – or a digitally delivered text from the internet?

One key difference is that, in other forms of communication, various interpreters come between the author and the audience. In film, for example, there are producers, a director, actors, sound, lighting, set and costume designers, a music director, special effects engineers, and an editor. Every one of them has a view – an interpretation – that predominates. Everything in the making of a film is done to present that interpretation to the audience. This is so with plays on stage, TV and radio, and every kind of broadcast programme, including the 'news'.

Even when a text is read aloud the same thing is happening: the reader-aloud is interpreting the text for the listeners.

But when we read a book to ourselves we are on our own. We are the most in charge of the interpretation as it is possible to be. We must be our own producer, director, actors, etc. Which is why reading a book is the most difficult, the most testing form of communication. We should never underestimate the skill and experience involved. The pleasure is more hard-won than the pleasure of listening to radio or watching a film or stage play or TV drama.

Books are individual objects, but similar in kind, just as human beings are individuals and yet are like each other in kind. Books have an integrity that must not be abused.

DIGITAL TEXTS

Texts delivered electronically have no integrity. The computer is a device engineered for interference. If you know how to do it, all electronic texts can easily be changed by the reader *and are meant to be*. It is in the nature of the beast.

And though texts on a screen are called pages, they are not the same as pages in a book. They are only pages in the sense that there is a limit to the amount of a text that can be displayed on a screen. And you can alter how much is on a screen by changing the size of the letters and the length of the line.

To put it at its simplest, whatever an author may have intended, everything can be changed by the recipient and no one thinks it is wrong to do so.

Nor does the reader of a text on a screen have any sense of the length of the whole text. When you hold in your hand the thousand or so pages of *War and Peace* you have a visceral sense of how long the story is, the kind of time and energy you'll need to read it, *and this is part of the experience of reading it*. You don't have that knowledge or experience with a digital text, even when it is delivered as an eBook for use with an eReader.

Which brings us to a distinction we need to make between digital texts delivered to a computer and those delivered in such a way that the text cannot be tampered with and the book pages and their sequence cannot be altered, as is the case at present with eReaders, the only purpose of which is to read a book in electronic rather than paper-print form. Of course, you still don't have any sense of the length of the book. But as the device is developed it is being made to resemble a paper-print book more and more. For example, in the first models there was only one screen which displayed only one page. Later models were designed to present two facing pages as in a paper book. At first there was only black and white line. Later versions included colour and half tone.

However, it is also the case that you can alter the amount of text on an eReader page. Sometimes, perhaps mostly, this doesn't matter because the author didn't deliberately intend each page of her book to be precisely one length of text. And so long as none of the text can be changed or deleted the essential integrity of the author's text is maintained. But when the author intended the page to be of a precise length – as, for example, in many picture books – then electronic delivery is right when it preserves the intended page, but is no longer a book when it does not.

IN SUM

The difference between a book and all other means of delivering a text is contained in the definition of a book. Whatever the means of delivery of a text, if it obeys the essential elements of the definition we can call it a book. If the text does not conform to the definition, then it isn't a book, and the experience of reading it will be different.

The book as a form embodies values and experiences special to itself. Until now, this was assumed because the Book was the predominant form of written communication. The changes in written communication brought about by electronic and digital technology now make it necessary to teach what a Book is and the differences between the Book and all other forms of communication.

(A more extensive treatment of this topic, titled 'The Future of the Book', is included in a collection of my essays, *Reading Talk*, pages 157-70, Thimble Press, 2001.)

17

The Enabling Adult

Previous chapters have described how adults can enable children to become readers. This chapter is about adults helping themselves.

Readers are made by readers. This is the main fact to keep in mind. A great deal depends, therefore, on how much we read and what we read. Inevitably and unconsciously, we try to make other people into the kind of reader we are ourselves. We will try to interest them in the kind of books we like the most. We lead them to think and talk about what they've read in the same way that we think and talk. And without saying anything at all, our behaviour communicates the place and importance reading holds in our own private lives. Therefore:

Know yourself as a reader. Tell yourself your reading history, write it down if this helps, and think about what it means in relation to learning readers.

I know, for instance, that I was born into a house where little reading of any kind went on but where there was a lot of storytelling – local gossip turned into dramatic or funny episodes told by my father, local folk tales told by my grandfather, Aesop's stories told by my mother. I know that I didn't learn to 'read' till I was nine – I remember the moment it happened – but I had an infant-school teacher who read aloud to us every day. And with hindsight I know that hearing so many stories at home and hearing so many books read aloud at school before I could read for myself, made me into the kind of reader I am now: one who hears every word in his head while he reads, as if someone is telling the story. Which means that as much as anything I enjoy the drama of narrative – the characters talking in voices of their own, the narrator telling what is happening, the pace and colour of the text. I also know that it was only because a friend insisted I go to the local library with him that I found out rather late (I was eleven) that there were thousands of books for young readers and that I could have any of them I wanted. It was only because a couple of secondary school teachers talked about books as if they mattered that I learned that reading literature was more than a pastime occupation. And it was a book I found for myself when I was fifteen, *Sons and Lovers* by D. H. Lawrence, that at last showed me how literature included me, that I could find myself there, the life I knew and a life I could hope to live.

Equally, it is by keeping track of what I read that I discover my prejudices. I don't much care for historical fiction, for example. And I take particular pleasure in the formal techniques of narrative, to the extent that I'm often more interested in how a story is told than I am in its content. Because I know this, I know I need the help of readers who enjoy historical fiction when I'm choosing books for a school library or classroom so that my prejudice doesn't warp the selection, and I need to listen carefully to what other people have to say about the content of a story if I'm to enjoy a fuller understanding of a text than I can manage on my own. I also know that it is never too late to become a serious reader, but that this is hard if you've no regular background of being read to or haven't many books near at hand, waiting till you're ready for them.

Most of all, I know that without enabling adults who are thoughtful readers to give you guidance, it is all but impossible to become a thoughtful literary reader yourself.

Protect your time to read. To keep fresh, and refreshed, as enablers of others, we have to continue extending ourselves – by taking a chance with authors we haven't come across before, books of a kind we aren't familiar with or find difficult. Yet, ironically, being a teacher or librarian or parent – more so, a full-time professional as well as a parent – leaves little time to sit quietly and read with energetic concentration for long enough or regularly enough to keep up with all the reading we know we'd like to do.

I don't pretend to have the answer – at least, not while our education system is run as it is. But I do know of some possibilities that have helped other people. Before I mention them, however, I want to make a further point.

Teachers are the professional group who take care of the entire population of young people, and who are professionally responsible for helping children become readers. If they entered their profession with a well-grounded, wide knowledge of the literature published for children, and with a trained understanding of how to bring it to the young, not only would the teaching of 'reading' be much more effective, but teachers would have a knowledge of books to sustain them and give them something to build on during the early years of their careers.

The message to any pre-service student must be: read as much as you can now, because you'll never have such a good chance again.

Besides, every child has only one go at being a child, only one go at being five, six, seven and so on. The first class you meet can be what they are now and never again. They can't wait while you discover the books you should tell them about and show them. You need that kind of working knowledge from the first day you're with them. If your training institution isn't helping you, ask why not. And meanwhile exercise your professional responsibility as best you can, on your own and along with other students who understand how important it is. Seek help from teachers and librarians who know what you're talking about. Some of the suggestions below will help you too.

Keep in touch. As always, everything begins with selection. When we have little time to read, it is more than ever important that we make informed choices. How can we do this best?

- Make sure you have regular access to specialist review sources. Newspaper reviews of books for the young are far too erratic and ad hoc to be much use. We need the help of well-edited journals, paper or online, covering books chosen from the full range of those published. There are now many online sources available.

- Handle the recent books. Reviews are useful but not enough in themselves if you're to make a properly informed judgement. The best way to do this is to read the reviews, list the books you think you most want to consider and then visit, say twice a year, or once a term, a place where you can see the full range of recently published books.

- Any school that takes its reading life seriously will make sure that one or preferably more of its staff have at least half a day twice a year to visit such a collection and come back with information and suggestions. At the very least, this should be counted as in-service training and time very well spent.

- Of course, more frequent visits to a good public children's library are useful, though inevitably you'll be limited to whatever happens to be left unborrowed on the shelves.

Help each other. No matter how dedicated we are, most of us need the support of other like-minded people if we are to keep up our enthusiasm and, just as important, if we are to go on developing as readers. Apart from the informal support from friends and colleagues in day-to-day contacts, there are three main forums where this can happen:

- *Staff meetings*. There should be at least once-a-term staff meetings where the reading life of the school is discussed, where new books are reviewed, and where the main aim is simply to share reading enthusiasms. Perhaps one book that has been read by everyone in time for the meeting can be discussed in detail in order to respond at our own level in the way we help our children respond at theirs.

- *Reading groups*. Join or help organize a group of, say, six or eight people who are interested in children's reading and who are willing to meet perhaps once every three months to share their own reading, both of books for children and of books they've read for themselves. It's a good thing if the members include keen parents as well as teachers and librarians from the area. The mix brings different perspectives to the booktalk.

- *In-service courses*. One of the most useful aspects of in-service courses that deal with children's reading is the impetus they provide for the members to give more time than they usually feel they should to topping up their knowledge of books. As one teacher put it: 'I tell my family, "Hard luck, you'll have to see to yourselves this evening, I've got my course work to do" and off I go to my bedroom and read so that I'm prepared for the next meeting, and I don't feel guilty about it!'

  (That people feel guilty at all when reading literature, whether for themselves or as part of their job, is in itself interesting. The same people don't feel guilty when marking pupils' work, or preparing audio-visual aids. Why do they feel guilt about reading, and what does this say about the priorities in our education system and our society?)

  If there are no in-service courses of this kind on offer, gather support from other teachers and demand them.

Help yourself. Some private aids help keep you going as a reader on your own:

- *Keep a reading diary!* I discussed this in Chapter 8. It's worth mentioning again, this time to make the point that the act of keeping a diary stimulates you to keep reading. You notice any falling off and that gives you the incentive to find out why and to do something about it.

- Make a simple rule about how many children's books you'll aim to get through regularly. Set a manageable number. (I'm a very slow reader, so it isn't any use setting myself a children's novel a week besides the other books I want to read, because I won't keep it up and then I'll feel I've failed. When teaching full-time, I found I could manage one every two weeks. There were periods when I could manage more, but that rule was a discipline that saw me through the times when I wouldn't have bothered otherwise.)

What is it that enabling adults, teachers especially, do? They provide, stimulate, demonstrate and respond.

They provide books and time to read them and an attractive environment where people want to read. They stimulate a desire to become a thoughtful reader. They demonstrate by reading aloud and by their own behaviour what a 'good' reader does. And they respond, and help others respond, to the individuality of everyone in the reading community they belong to.

In the Afterword to *Actual Minds, Possible Worlds* Jerome Bruner writes:

> I have tried to make the case that the function of literature as art is to open us to dilemmas, to the hypothetical, to the range of possible worlds that a text can refer to. I have used the term 'to subjunctivize', to render the world less fixed, less banal, more susceptible to recreation. Literature subjunctivizes, makes strange, renders the obvious less so, the unknowable less so as well, matters of value more open to reason and intuition. Literature, in this spirit, is an instrument of freedom, lightness, imagination, and yes, reason. It is our only hope against the long gray night.

By creating a reading environment of the kind I've described we can help children discover in literature this spirit of freedom and imagination.

PART TWO

Tell Me

Children, Reading & Talk

The goal is not to pack into our travelling bag only the best that has been thought and said but to find forms of critical talk that will improve the range or depth or precision of our appreciations...a kind of conversation that might get somewhere – not just a sharing of subjective opinions but a way of learning from one another . . .

Wayne C. Booth, *The Company We Keep*

The written word can fall into the hands of any knave or fool. Only in certain kinds of personal converse can we thoroughly clarify each other's understanding.

Iris Murdoch, *Metaphysics as a Guide to Morals*

A new description of reading could change what reading is; it should certainly change the way we look at it . . . Suppose we now began to speak of reading in terms of dialogue and desire; would that not be a better beginning?

Margaret Meek in *New Readings: Contributions to an Understanding of Literacy*

Note: Some of the books discussed by children in transcripts quoted in the following pages are out of print and may not be easy to obtain. I have tried, therefore, to choose extracts which do not require a detailed knowledge of the book in order to understand what is being said and how the children are responding. The main point is to keep your eye on the kinds of things the children say and how the teacher deals with the talk.

18

Introduction

Ours is a talkative age. Never before have people talked so much. The telephone, blogs, Twitter, text messages, radio, cinema, television, audio and digital recording have all increased our opportunities for speaking to one another not only when we are together but across distance and across time as well. Children used to be taught to be seen but not heard. Now adults are criticized for not listening enough to children, who are encouraged in school and out to speak their minds.

These days we are all judged by how articulate we are – not that we talk any better or listen any more carefully than did people in less voluble times.

Tell Me is about helping children to talk well about books. And not only talk well but listen well. (What I mean by 'well' will become apparent, I hope, along the way.) And talk well not just about books but about any text from one-word signs to the writing we call literature, which is the kind of text I shall be concentrating on.

I am not interested in talk for its own sake but in the part talk plays in the lives of discriminating, thoughtful, pleasure-taking readers. I also believe that talk is essential in our lives, not least because most of us, as the saying goes, do not know what we think till we hear what we say. Provided, that is, we know how to talk well rather than simply spilling out words in the kind of thoughtless blether that gets us nowhere.

Talking well about books is a high-value activity in itself. But talking well about books is also the best rehearsal there is for talking well about other things. So in helping children to talk about their reading, we help them to be articulate about the rest of their lives.

In a talkative age, what could be more useful?

I once visited a class of ten-year-olds in Canada who talked so well about their reading that an astonished visiting educator asked their teacher for her lesson notes. 'Well,' she replied, 'if you take me and all the books in our classroom, and let me do with your children what I've done with these over the last few months, you'll have my lesson notes.'

Teaching readers, whether children or adults, how to talk well isn't achieved in a few days. Nor is it a programmatic business that can be expressed in mechanical one-two-three lesson notes that anyone can use successfully. Even writing about it at length is not satisfactory. The fact is we learn to talk well by doing it with people who already know how, just as we learn best the way to teach by working with an experienced teacher. As readers, as talkers, as teachers we are all apprentices. And as with all the executive arts based on craft skill, the only thing I can usefully do is to offer practical information, explain some of the processes, and outline the ground rules developed by experienced practitioners. The rest (the art and essence) can only be learned by doing. There is no quick way, and there is no way but practice.

In my experience the best place to begin is with ourselves, as readers and as talkers. I was one of a small group of teachers who set out to improve our teaching of children as readers, when we discovered how important talk is in that process. Out of this developed what has become known as the 'Tell me' approach.

Please note: an approach – not a method, not a system, not a schematic programme. Not a rigid set of rules, but simply a way of asking particular kinds of question which each of us can adapt to suit our personality and the needs of our students.

This book has grown from that base, refined and expanded by further work by myself and by other teachers who have reported their experiences to me – from those working in infant school through primary and secondary school and college to tutors of postgrads and in-service teachers.

Of course all practical teaching needs to be carefully grounded in theory. The 'Tell me' approach grew out of the lessons learned from studying the phenomenology of reading (Wolfgang Iser helped us here), along with reader-response theory, the insights offered by feminist critics (especially what they say about co-operative discourse), and the writing of various thinkers, including especially Roland Barthes, Jonathan Culler, Jerome Bruner, Margaret Meek, and Wayne C. Booth.

One more point by way of introduction. There is a correlation between the richness of the reading environment in which readers live and the richness of their talk about what they've read. As explained in Part One, children who are surrounded by a well-displayed stock of appropriate and knowledgeably chosen books, who are read aloud to every day, who are expected to read for themselves just as often, and who are encouraged to gossip informally to each other and to their teachers about their reading, are well prepared to engage in the kind of formal talk we're thinking about here. Those not so well looked after are unlikely to respond as readily to the 'Tell me' approach.

Any teacher who plunges headlong into 'Tell me' sessions, and finds things aren't going well, shouldn't blame the approach before considering the reading history and the reading environment of the students *and the teacher* involved.

19

'TELL ME' BEGINNINGS

Where does talk 'fit' into what some specialists call the 'reading process'? And what kind of talk do I mean?

When I first drew the Reading Circle (page 15) many years ago it did not include the elements of 'Formal talk' and 'Book gossip'. We hadn't realized then that these had a place. But over the years, as colleagues and I looked more closely at the whole process, we became aware that it was like a map drawn by people who thought the reading world was flat.

This is how we saw it: Suppose a child selects a story by Enid Blyton (or any other very prolific writer who has produced all kinds of story from the very simplest books for babies to novels aimed at adolescents), settles down and reads it, enjoys it so much that he or she finds another by the same author, reads it, finds another, and so on. According to our map we were observing a reader, someone many teachers would count a success. But of course we were uneasy. Exclusively repetitious reading of any one kind of book, of any one writer, is flat-earth reading. The reader may never know about (or, worse still, may not want to acknowledge) the world as round, plural, disparate, many-faceted.

Flat-earthers resist any invitation to explore beyond the boundaries of familiar territory because of the fearsome dangers they are sure lie in wait at the edge of their world. One of these dangers is called boredom. Another is called difficulty. A third is fear of exhaustion (perhaps the journey round the other side – if there is another side! – will never end). There are many other fears well known to enabling adults.

'I couldn't get past the first page / chapter.'
'It isn't my kind of book.'
'It looks long. I'll never get through it.'
'I don't like the cover / title / author / blurb / hardbacks / paperbacks / print / paper / feel / smell.'
'There aren't any pictures. / I don't like the pictures.'
'There are a lot of hard words.'
'I don't have time.'
Et cetera.

What is it that changes people from being flat-earth into not just round-earth but intergalactic readers? How do we turn a narrow-minded closed circle into an open-minded spiral that transports us into the multifarious universe of literature?

Our study group asked these questions of ourselves. We were fairly typical of the people we taught. We had all been brought up in conventional working-class and lower-middle-class homes. We had all attended neighbourhood schools, where we had met the variety of competence and incompetence always to be found in such places. Some of us were late developers as readers, others were avid devotees from infancy. Some of us had been flat-earthers and had changed.

Were there any common denominators in our experience? Had anything particularly helped us? Indeed, were we open-minded readers ourselves? And what kept us spiralling now?

We quickly found some shared answers.

As children we had all been affected, and still were, by what others whom we liked, respected, and would listen to, said about books they had read, and which we then read because of their encouragement. And we had all been affected, and still were, by what we found ourselves saying during everyday conversation about what we'd read.

It was in what other people told us about their reading, and what we told of our own, that we thought we had discovered the heart of the matter. A certain kind of booktalk gave us the information we needed, the energy, the impetus, the will to explore beyond our familiar boundaries. We could all recount memories of people who were particularly important in our lives for this reason, some of them teachers. We could all remember moments of booktalk that sent our reading another turn up the literary spiral.

Try asking the same questions of yourself and a group of trusted colleagues and see if your experience matches ours.

Quite obviously, however, not all talk – and not everybody's talk – works like that. What kinds of talk, and which special features in it, are affective?

We began to listen to people when they were gossiping about their reading. We examined theories of reading and reader response. And the more we studied the more we became convinced of the essential part talk plays in even the most sophisticated reader's reading life, never mind the centrally important part it plays in learning-children's lives. (Can you imagine any child becoming a reader if no one ever said anything to him about all the books he could choose from, and all those marks on pages that he was trying to read?) This is what a colleague, Steve Bicknell, once wrote to me:

> At our last meeting you said, 'The act of reading lies in talking about what you have read.' Looking back through my notes of conversations I've participated in with children, I constantly return to a remark made by eight-year-old Sarah (not usually noted for her willingness to risk an opinion in front of her class): 'We don't know what we think about a book until we've talked about it.'

It was perhaps provocative rather than entirely accurate of me to locate the act of reading in the act of talking, but Sarah certainly spoke a truth we recognized.

If you eavesdrop on people's book gossip you won't find their talk following a logical agenda, but if you analyse a transcript of it the subject matter can be divided into three broad categories which I call 'The Three Sharings'.

20

The Three Sharings

SHARING ENTHUSIASMS

When friends start talking about a book it's usually because one of them wants to share her enthusiasm. 'I've just read this amazing book,' she says. 'Have you read it?'

We all know the variations on that opening ploy, and how the conversation then continues. If others in the group haven't read the book, they want to know what it's about. But what does 'about' mean? Most people simply reply by describing the plot and the characters or the story's setting. What they don't talk about is significance. They tend to say something like: 'Oh, it's about these three older men who go off on a sailing trip leaving their families behind and then' . . . Much less often they say: 'It's a novel about family politics and the strains of family life in a post-feminist society.' That is, they do not summarize meaning as an academic critic would. Rather they tend to retell the story and talk about what they liked and didn't like – which might be anything from the nature of the story and characters and setting to the form, the way it is told.

If the others have read the book, the talk tends to slip at once into the kind of sharing that begins with such ploys as: 'Did you like the part where . . .' or 'Didn't you think it was very funny when . . .'

In everyday gossip, people seem to delay discussion of meaning (interpretation and significance) till they have heard what their friends have to say. In other words, the meaning of a story emerges from the conversation; it isn't set up at the start and then discussed, which is what often happens in formal academic booktalk.

These book-reading friends are sharing two kinds of enthusiasm:

- *likes*: enthusiasms about the elements in the story that have pleased and attracted, surprised and impressed them and made them want to go on reading;

- *dislikes*: aversions to elements of the story that displeased them, or put them off reading for one reason or another.

It is important to understand that readers are often as vehement about what they've disliked as about what they've liked. You see the effect of this in the gossip. If friends like the same things and find themselves in complete agreement, the gossip is often less interesting and ends sooner than if there are elements that inspire opposing responses.

SHARING PUZZLES (I.E. DIFFICULTIES)

A reader will often express a dislike for elements of the story that have puzzled him – things he has found difficult to understand. 'What did it mean when . . .' he'll say, or: 'Did you understand the bit where . . . ' Sometimes we hide our puzzlement in such comments as, 'I didn't like the way the story ended, did you?' or 'I wasn't convinced by the teacher as a character, were you?' or 'What was it you liked so much about the scene where . . . ?'

One of the friends will try to provide an answer. (How this is done is considered below in 'Sharing connections'.) It is in this part of the talk that meaning – an interpretation of the story – is most obviously being negotiated. The friends discuss the puzzle and the suggested explanation, and out of this comes an understanding of (or an agreement to disagree on) what the text is 'about' – what it 'means' – to that group of readers at that time.

I say 'that group of readers at that time' because a different group of readers might discover a different interpretation, a different emphasis of meaning. As indeed might the same group if they talked about the same book at a later date. The meanings of any text shift according to the context of the readers' own lives and their needs at a particular time.

If you doubt this, look, for instance, at the apparently simple word EXIT. In a cinema or restaurant or any other place where the word is used as a sign above a door, you would expect it to mean 'This is the way out' and wouldn't think twice about reading it like that if you wanted to leave.

In an aeroplane when in flight, the word is used as a sign above doors. But we know better than to use it, even if we feel very much like leaving the aircraft, because we know that, at that time and in that place, to do so means death.

If significant shifts in contextualized meaning can inhabit such an apparently simple word as this – a word we try to use as unambiguously as possible – how much more likely it is that a story using many words in deliberately ambiguous ways, as all stories do, will be laden with meanings whose potential becomes actual according to what different readers in different groups at different times and places discover together. Which is why we now accept that, as Frank Kermode wrote, 'the illusion of the single right reading is possible no longer'. In any text, no matter how simple, there is always the possibility of multiple meanings.

In sharing and solving difficulties over the puzzling elements of a story we may discover what that piece of writing means for each of us now.

SHARING CONNECTIONS (I.E. DISCOVERING PATTERNS)

We solve puzzles, we resolve difficulty, by finding significant connections between one element in a text and another: elements, for example, of language, motifs, events, characters, symbols and so on.

Human beings cannot bear chaos, meaninglessness, confusion. We constantly look for connectedness, for patterns of relationship between one thing and another that make a meaning we can understand. And if we can't find a pattern, we tend to construct one out of the disparate odds and ends of raw material in front of us. We do this with everything in our lives, and we do it as we read.

We can only 'read' when we are able to recognize in the marks on the page the patterns called words and sentences. But learning to read stories isn't only a matter of learning to recognize these verbal patterns; it is also a matter of learning to recognize the formal, narrative patterns of the story itself.

Think of it like this: a building is made of brick and stone and wood and steel, which we can identify when we see them. But these materials are used to create a pattern of shapes that make rooms of different kinds, and stairs and roofs and windows and doors, which in turn create different kinds of building – a house, an office block, a factory, a school – which we also learn to identify from our experience of knowing how each is used. Texts are the same. They are built of different elements of language used in various ways to create different kinds of texts. We learn to look for details of design constructed in patterns that tell us what kind of building, what kind of story we have in front of us.

When the 'Tell me' approach is being used, children sometimes have trouble understanding what we mean by 'patterns'. Try drawing their attention to the story patterns in familiar folk tales (the three sons, the third one of which performs three tests in order to win the prize, for example; the repeated 'I'll huff and I'll puff and I'll blow your house down' in 'The Three Little Pigs'); the patterns of rhythm and rhyme in a limerick; and the visual patterns in illustrations and decoration that help us 'make sense' of a picture. They'll soon catch on and extend the range of their pattern-finding.

Not that all the patterns come from the text itself. There are extra-textual patterns that can be brought to the reader's aid. Two of these and another, third, element are important in booktalk and the making of meaning:

- Critics call the first one *world-to-text*. This means comparing the events or characters or language of a story with events or people or language known personally to the reader. We bring our own world to the world of the text and by comparing them discover meanings in one or the other or in both.

- In the same way readers sometimes *compare one text with another*. They describe how one book is like another or how it differs. Or they compare a character in one story with a character in another, understanding both a little better by thinking about their similarities and differences.

- Both of these comparisons rely on *memory*: memory of our own lives, memory of other texts we've read. The play of memory provoked by a text is an integral part of the experience of reading and a source of its pleasure. Very often in ordinary book gossip all the talk will be concentrated on the memories the book has brought to mind.

These features in book gossip do not occur in any formal order. They are mixed up as the talk meanders about, apparently without conscious arrangement. In fact, the talk is guided by immediate need: the need to express satisfactions, or dissatisfactions, the need to articulate new thoughts in order to hear what they sound like, the need to 'bring out' disturbing elements provoked by the story so that we can externalize them – hold them up, so to speak, look at them and thus gain some control over them. Like ordinary gossip, 'Tell me' booktalk is not orderly and linear, not what some specialists call 'totalizing discourse'. It is not the sort of discussion that looks for specific answers to questions asked in a prescribable order, one question 'logically' following another.

In essence, talking about literature is a form of shared contemplation. Booktalk is a way of giving form to the thoughts and emotions stimulated by the book and by the meaning(s) we make together out of its text – the imaginatively controlled messages sent from the author that we interpret in whatever way we find useful or delightful.

21

Four Kinds of Saying

Booktalk isn't just one person communicating something straightforwardly to another. It is a more complicated and more communal activity than that. There are various motivations and various functions simultaneously at work. Much has been written about the role and practice of talk in learning. This is how one of the research-writers, Gordon Wells, expresses the central point:

> What seems to be important is that, to be most helpful, the child's experience of conversation should be in a one-to-one situation in which the adult is talking about matters that are of interest and concern to the child, such as what he or she is doing, has done, or plans to do, or about activities in which the child and adult engage together. The reason for this is the fact that, when both child and adult are engaged in a shared activity, the chances are maximised that they will be attending to the same objects and events and interpreting the situation in similar ways. This means they will each have the best chance of correctly interpreting what the other says and so of being able collaboratively to build up a shared structure of meaning about the topic that is the focus of their intersubjective attention.

The 'Tell me' approach tries to build on this basic conversational mode, enlarging the partners from one-to-one, child-and-adult, to an enabling adult with a community of readers whose mutual interest is focused by a shared text. As an activity 'Tell me' booktalk is individual and at the same time communal and co-operative. Each participant must listen to what others have to say and take account of what everyone else thinks.

Every time we speak, we say something that we hear for ourselves. I think of this as a private speech act. But when we speak we usually involve one or more others because we want to communicate something. I think of this as a public speech act. So talking is both private and public. Any analysis of this sort is of course artificial. Talk doesn't feel like this in life. But for teachers who try to help children talk well it is useful to have some grasp of the intricate weaving of motivation and effect that provokes speech and rewards listening.

SAYING FOR YOURSELF

The private motivation for this speech act is the need to hear said what has been so far only inwardly thought, because, as is often repeated, 'we don't know what we think till we hear what we say'. Speech is part of the thought process, sometimes indicated by such remarks as: 'I'm only thinking aloud' or 'Let me try this on you' or 'How does this sound?' Saying something out loud can tell us whether or not we know what we're thinking about.

But saying out loud usually involves a listener. And the involvement of others somehow alters our understanding of what we are saying and makes us think even harder about it. So the public motivation for 'thinking out loud' is not just to hear what we are thinking but also to help clarify what we mean in a way we cannot on our own. However, the involvement of others engages a second kind of saying.

SAYING TO OTHERS

Whether we speak to clarify our own minds for ourselves, or in order to communicate our thoughts to another person (or, most likely, to do both at once), the saying of a thought to someone else means that the listener has to interpret what has been said. The listener reflects on it and reflects it back to the speaker. Then we see what we've said 'in a different light'.

Let me show this happening even in the writing of these paragraphs. In the first letter-to-colleagues version of this essay published in *Booktalk* I called this section 'Levels of Saying' and under the subheading 'Saying for Others' wrote '. . . the saying of a thought to someone else means that the listener has now thought it too . . . the public effect is to make our thoughts into corporately owned possessions'.

During a chance meeting Gordon Wells showed me how 'Levels of Saying' was misleading because it suggested that one level must be superior to another – and he was sure that I did not mean to imply this. He was right. None of what I now, as a result of Wells's comment, call the 'Kinds of Saying' is more important than the others. They are interrelated, not a hierarchy of less valuable rising to more.

In saying to others, then, the private motivation is the hope that they will interpret what we have said and help us understand it better. The public effect is that by pooling our thoughts we extend our individual ability to think. This is the basis of a think-tank.

Steve Bicknell provided an example of this second kind of saying from the early days of his work with the 'Tell me' approach in a lesson with some eight-year-olds.

> We were talking about Sendak's *Where the Wild Things Are* and things weren't particularly interesting. Nobody had mentioned dreams or imagination; we were still busy with likes and dislikes. To move things on I asked them to tell me about what they didn't understand. Some immediately began comparing illustrations and saying that they couldn't understand how trees would grow in Max's room. I said, 'Yes, that's certainly a bit strange.' Wayne replied, 'He's having a dream.' Several 'Oh, yeah's' followed and some looked even more confused. I asked for a show of hands. 'Who agrees with Wayne?' The majority agreed and claimed they had always known it to be a dream! Wayne had actually, I think, enabled the others to possess what he had said and, also, by saying it had made others convinced that they had already thought it.

SAYING TOGETHER

The private motivation for joining in discussion is a conscious attempt to sort out with other people problems we recognize are too difficult and complex for anyone to sort out alone.

The public effect of this conscious pooling of thought is that we come to a 'reading' – a knowledge, understanding, appreciation – of a book that far exceeds what any one member of the group could have achieved alone. Each member knows some part of it, but no one knows it all. And the members of the 'community of readers' knowingly apply themselves to a co-operative act of discussion aimed at discovering more about the text than would otherwise be possible.

SAYING THE NEW

The private motivation here is the desire to engage in booktalk for the sake of the activity itself, because we have learned not only that 'saying together' produces an interpretation built of the segments of understanding we can offer individually but also that the talk itself often generates new understandings, increased appreciations, that no one till then could have articulated. The sensation is of 'lift off', of flight into the hitherto unknown: the experience of revelation. By closely attending together, we are rewarded with riches of meaning in the text we did not know it offered before we first shared our individual understandings.

Lissa Paul reports that her undergrads talk about the 'intellectual pleasure' they get from turning back to a text repeatedly in order to interpret it – and how much they enjoy discovering textual secrets. My own experience is that children obtain similar intellectual pleasure from this activity too.

The public effect of so productive an experience is that people come to know the social importance of literary reading. (Once known never forgotten and ever after wished for.) They discover at first hand how reading – the whole experience of the 'reading circle' – transcends pastime entertainment, bedtime cosiness, or everyday functional value: how, rather, it offers us images to think with and a means of creating and re-creating the very essence of our individual and corporate lives. (There are some who would say, complain even, that this is to invest literary discourse –

reading and 'serious' talk about it – with a metaphysical if not a religious significance. But then, I believe it has.)

When you think about these distinctions in relation to the practical business of teaching children to talk well about their reading, some questions immediately suggest themselves which you may want to discuss with your colleagues:

Saying for yourself. What kind of preparation helps us think about our reading? What questions can we ask each other that help release thoughts rather than inhibit them?

Saying to others. People may hear but this does not necessarily mean that they listen. Telling our thoughts is a waste of time if others don't wish to listen to what we're saying but only hear what they'd like us to say. What helps us listen attentively? What helps children make the move from egotistic speakers to co-operative listeners?

Saying together. Because we say and listen, does this mean we 'know'? Does understanding have to be articulated? Does co-operative talk help us say more than we thought we knew and, by hearing what others then say, make us aware of what we didn't know we knew?

In *Philosophy and the Young Child*, to which this writing owes a debt, Gareth B. Matthews tells an anecdote about a child edging up to this problem:

> Some question of fact arose between James and his father, and James said, 'I know it is!' His father replied, 'But perhaps you might be wrong!' Dennis [four years seven months] then joined in, saying, 'But if he knows, he can't be wrong! *Thinking*'s sometimes wrong, but *knowing*'s always right.'

You may be 'right' but do you know what you've actually said? Because someone utters an incisive comment, does this mean she knows what she means? She senses it is right, intuition says she is, but is that enough? And even if she is completely aware in her own mind of the implications of the statement, is this the case with all those who heard the statement, no matter how attentively they listened? What does the teacher do to consolidate knowing in both speaker and listeners? And how is this done without spoiling the pleasure of reading or the clarity of saying?

Saying the new. What does the teacher say or do when booktalk stimulates a 'new' thought? And how do we know a 'new' thought when we hear one? For we must remember that the 'newness' we have in mind relates to children's understanding, not our own. Though the experience of every teacher who listens attentively to pupils is that they give the teacher new thoughts too.

All this may be true, but does reading literature and discussing it deserve so much attention during precious time-short school days? At the end of *Actual Minds, Possible Worlds* Jerome Bruner offers the hope that 'a new breed of developmental theory' will arise, the central technical concern of which

> will be how to create in the young an appreciation of the fact that many worlds are possible, that meaning and reality are created and not discovered, that negotiation is the art of constructing new meanings by which individuals can regulate their relations with each other. It will not, I think, be an image of human development that locates all of the sources of change inside the individual, the solo child.

A few pages later Bruner shows us why literature and discourse about it lie at the heart of this development.

> I have tried to make the case that the function of literature as art is to open us to dilemmas, to the hypothetical, to the range of possible worlds that a text can refer to. I have used the term 'to subjunctivize,' to render the world less fixed, less banal, more susceptible to recreation. Literature subjunctivizes, makes strange, renders the obvious less so, the unknowable

> less so as well, matters of value more open to reason and intuition. Literature, in this spirit, is an instrument of freedom, lightness, imagination, and yes, reason. It is our only hope against the long gray night . . . What will see us through is the writing of poems and novels that help perpetually to recreate the world, and the writing of criticism and interpretation that celebrate the varied ways in which human beings search for meaning and for its incarnation in reality – or better, in such rich realities as we can create.

The point I want to emphasize is the central place of talk in the critical activity Bruner describes. The kind of talk I am dealing with here has traditionally been called 'criticism'. Which causes sceptics to question whether children can be critics.

22

Are Children Critics?

When our study group asked teacher colleagues this question the answer was often No. Criticism, we were assured, is an unnatural, specialist and adult activity for which you need training as well as a perverse taste for pleasure-destroying analysis. Criticism, these teachers seemed to believe, deals in abstractions, in unfeeling intellectualism, calculating dissection. You can't 'do' criticism with children, they said, and if you try you only put them off literature altogether. Many of them, it turned out, had been put off by what they thought of as criticism during secondary-school and tertiary literature courses.

We asked the question in the first place because our work had persuaded us that children possess an innate critical faculty. They instinctively question, report, compare and judge. Left to themselves, they make their opinions and feelings plain, and are interested in the feelings of their friends. When they talk about books, films, television, sport, or whatever own-time activities they share enthusiastically, they enjoy gathering information and are quite as discriminating as an adult connoisseur. No one, for example, is more critical than a ten-year-old soccer fan comparing notes about the previous night's game, or is more trenchant in defence of strongly held opinions.

If there is a deep interest in a subject, and the facilities are provided for its expression, children are, it seemed to us self-evident, natural critics from quite early ages (certainly by the time they start school). What our dissenting colleagues were talking about, we decided, was a warped notion of literary criticism based upon their own unhappy experiences.

What, then, was our own view of literary criticism? What do critics do? And is that what children do or can be enabled to do?

It is difficult to persuade any academic literary critic to sum up briefly what criticism is. J. A. Cuddon's *Dictionary of Literary Terms* says, 'The art or science of literary criticism is devoted to the comparison and analysis, to the interpretation and evaluation of works of literature.' But so narrow a description would leave many contemporary critics greatly discomfited. What we all know, however, is that criticism has to do with meaning in texts, with 'making sense' of them – stating it, finding it, agreeing and disagreeing about it. Interpretation is part of what criticism is. So too is a consideration of how the meaning is made – by language, forms of narrative, conventions and ideologies – as well as what the reader does with the text and what the text does to the reader.

A simple truth underlies all this: criticism is autobiographical. Whatever the critic's specialist preference – linguistic, structuralist, feminist, political, psychoanalytical, and so on – the basis is the reader's own experience of the text. Without that there is nothing. Nothing to work on, nothing of interest. So, as Jonathan Culler put it in *On Deconstruction*, 'To speak of the meaning of the work is to tell a story of reading'. To this extent, because it is concerned with the reader's 'story of a reading', reader-response theory is a good place to begin, for anyone interested in children and criticism.

When we asked 'What does a critic do?' we decided that W. H. Auden's essay 'Reading', in *The Dyer's Hand and Other Essays*, was a sensible, down-to-earth basis for considering what children can or can't do. Auden wanted critics to:

1. Introduce me to authors or works of which I was hitherto unaware.

2. Convince me that I have undervalued an author or a work because I had not read them carefully enough.

3. Show me relations between works of different ages and cultures which I could never have seen for myself because I do not know enough and never shall.

4. Give a 'reading' of a work which increases my understanding of it.

5. Throw light upon the process of artistic 'Making'.

6. Throw light upon the relation of art to life, to science, economics, ethics, religion, etc.

23

Children Being Critics

Can children – do children – tell 'the story of their reading'? And do they ever do what Auden wanted of a critic? We began listening more carefully to what children said and reading more carefully what they wrote about books. We soon realized how much we do not notice, especially when working with large classes. Often children express themselves in rapid cut-and-thrust talk and the teacher, concerned as much with keeping order and saying what she wants to say as with what the children are saying, misses the kernels of thought peppered through the conversation. Besides, a lot of the best things are said in private, outside formal class discussion. You have to eavesdrop as well.

Here are some examples of children behaving as critics, whether in a formal or informal setting, in speech or writing.

WILLIAM, aged ten, when asked if he didn't find Arthur Ransome's stories 'rather long and slow' (I meant boring), replied, 'Arthur Ransome is the sort of writer you enjoy most after you've finished him.'

This carries a number of possible meanings, all of them pertinent. William might be saying: When you are reading a richly made story, you experience the greatest pleasure only when you've finished and can view the whole pattern of the book and see how everything fits together. He might also be saying: All reading requires an expenditure of time and effort, energy and stamina; books like Arthur Ransome's, because they are long and detailed, take so much time and energy that for a while you wonder whether it's worth going on; but if you persist and reach the end, you feel greater enjoyment because of the satisfaction that comes from 'seeing it through'.

If William meant something like this he was making a critically profound statement about reading itself, as well as about the nature of Ransome's novels. Of course, he might have been making a joke like the one about banging your head against a brick wall – that Ransome's books are so tedious the only pleasure comes when you stop reading. Which might be considered a critical comment of the same order as the others. As it is, we'll never know what he meant because I didn't ask him and, typically of a child, he didn't feel it necessary to explain. Had I overcome my surprise at such a sophisticated idea so succinctly put, what, if anything, should I have 'done' with it?

An aside about jokes: I've discovered, while working with the 'Tell me' approach, that nothing readers say during booktalk is wasted, least of all the jokes, which often take us to the heart of the matter quickly and surprisingly. If jokes are made, don't dismiss them; see where they lead.

HELEN, aged ten, when asked if she had found any 'boring bits' in my story, *The Present Takers*: 'I thought the first page and a half was boring and then I realized why it had to be.'

Helen's remark invites curiosity about what she means, yet no one asked her, neither myself nor the nine or ten other children in the group. Can she have understood that her boredom precisely matches the passages in the book that establish the kind of story it is going to be and how it should be read? Had she understood that literary boredom can be a matter of confusion, a period during reading when the reader is coming to grips with the demands of unfamiliar writing (the patch in a book that some readers call 'difficult')? If so, she had performed an astute act of criticism. Could she have explained more about her boredom and revealed more about it to herself and the rest of us? Then she would have been doing what Auden wants a critic to do in his point 4 – giving a 'reading' which increases our understanding of the book. On the other hand, she might have been wanting the rest of us to show her what she meant. Or did she only discover that she 'knew' what she meant when she said that sentence aloud, and did she wish to make her meaning clear so that she could understand her own thought?

My guess, after hearing many such comments and trying to help children explore them, is that children often do want to understand their own critical insights. What they expect the teacher to do is enable them to make the exploration. They expect her to help them articulate meaning, not by saying it for them, nor by explaining it to them, but by releasing their own ability to say it for themselves. Which begs one of the questions this book is trying to answer: What does the teacher do that enables child readers to speak for themselves?

MARK, described as a 'very limited ability' eight-year-old, after the teacher had asked if the class could find any patterns in *The Owl Who Was Afraid of the Dark* by Jill Tomlinson: 'There is a pattern in the way Plop goes along the branch each time, then falls off each time, and then meets another person each time.'

Mark is playing a game of 'I Spy' . He is discovering more or less hidden connections between various elements in the story, and finds enjoyment in doing so. A great deal of critical activity, even of the most sophisticated kind, is concerned with finding patterns – of language, of narrative 'codes', of plot, of images, of character, and the rest. Where we focus our attention – what we highlight – varies according to the nature of the story and the personal imperatives of any one reader's reading of it. But all the time our experience shows that by finding patterns we make meaning, and that when we make meaning we are rewarded with a feeling of pleasure. Mark may be of 'very limited ability' and only eight, but he is observant and precise in saying what he has noticed. Whatever his limitations were assumed to be, they were no impediment to the exercise of his innate critical faculty, given two conditions:

First, a choice of book on which his abilities could operate. The language, pictures, content of the story, and its form – the way of telling the story – were all familiar to him.

Second, a skilled and practised companion to whom he could apprentice himself as a reader and a critic, one who enabled him to talk, and who knew how to help him focus his attention. Mark's companion was our colleague Barbara Raven, who translated an 'adult' act of structural analysis into a 'child enticing' game of 'I Spy'.

SARAH, aged six, of *Railway Passage* by Charles Keeping: 'At the beginning some of the pictures are dull and at the end the pictures are coloured but one of the pictures isn't and that picture is one of Uncle Meanie and I think it is dark because it isn't happy.'

Sarah is learning to tell herself and her friends how stories work by looking at Keeping's subtly designed picture books, in which so many of the narrative codes are 'written' into the pictures. This way she is learning about literary complexity even before she can cope with linguistic complexity. And she is learning to do this with critical discrimination by saying what she has noticed, by listening to what others say, and by discussing their mutual observations.

I have not revealed what makes Sarah's saying even more striking. It was written. I have changed nothing except to provide capital letters for Uncle Meanie and an apostrophe for 'isn't'. Sarah would, however, have said what she had noticed to her teacher, Jill Hopes, and her classmates, before writing it down. And she had written what she wanted to say for a 'real purpose', not for the mere exercise of showing her teacher she could do it. All of this helped her sort out what she wanted to say and the best order of words to say it in before she tackled the task, difficult enough to require all her attention, of writing the words down. I was the 'real purpose' that provided the stimulus for such hard work. Sarah knew she was going to send her comments to an unknown adult, who had a genuine interest in her thoughts about Keeping's books. Sarah was one of the makers of *A Book All About Books* which accompanied an audiotape of the children talking about their reading of *Charley, Charlotte and the Golden Canary*, of *Joseph's Yard* and other picture books by Charles Keeping.

'The lion in *The Crane* [by Reiner Zimnik] is the same as the black and white rabbit in *Watership Down* [by Richard Adams],' Anna Collins reported one of her ten-year-old boys saying in a somewhat startling (and accurate?) example of children making connections and comparisons.

In an article in *Signal* 26, 'Them's for the Infants, Miss', Elaine Moss provided further tape-recorded evidence from eight- to eleven-year-olds talking about *Come Away from the Water, Shirley* by John Burningham when they said it is 'Like Peter Pan, Miss' 'No, like Captain Pugwash'. She also related how there were some children

> at every age who did not manage to make the jump across the 'gutter' from left-hand pages where the parents sit, occasionally addressing the unseen Shirley, to the right-hand pages on which Shirley is seen synthesizing a real rowing boat and stray dog on the shore into the fabric of her vivid daydream . . . But far more children, again at all ages, did make the jump and were intrigued by the clues John Burningham laid for them. Although Shirley is not seen on the left-hand pages, 'She must have been there or her mum and dad wouldn't have kept talkin' to her, would they?'; 'Her body was there for them to tell not to do things, like "Don't play with that dog, you don't know where he's been", but her think was with the pirates.'

Shirley's body being there for her parents to order about but her 'think' being with the pirates is a precise account of the story and the formal arrangement of the pictures across each doublespread that controls the narrative. That this was understood by children of all primary school ages, and by the majority of them, further confirms our conviction that everyone is born with a critical faculty. Helping children learn how to use this faculty with consciously ordered attention is what teachers are for.

'TELL ME' BEGINNERS

Here is an extract from a transcript of a young teacher, Susan Jayne Lamacq, at the beginning of her work (she was in her last year of undergraduate training at the time) learning how to use the 'Tell me' approach as she helps children talk about their reading, and discovering just how critically discerning their observations can be. The children are a mixed group, aged nine to eleven, in a small Oxfordshire primary school. When this passage was recorded Susan had been working with the class for six weeks, during which she and the children had become more and more confident in their booktalk as they learned to trust each other and to accept that everything was 'honourably reportable' (see page 133). The picture book they are discussing after a second reading is John Burningham's *Granpa*:

TEACHER: Has anybody noticed anything they want to tell us?

LEE: At the end he [Granpa] has gone.

BRYAN: Maybe he's gone to Africa without her.

GWILYM: She [the unnamed little girl] asks if worms go to heaven, she knows people do.

CANDY: Definitely.

JESSICA: He is gradually getting older and then he is very ill, then he dies.

TEACHER: Yes, I noticed that. Did anyone else?

GWILYM: It starts off as spring and goes all the way through.

TEACHER: Yes, starts in spring, through summer, autumn, and ends in winter. What do you think spring is like?

STUART: Growth, new life, cows have calves.

TEACHER: Brilliant!

GWILYM: The beginning of life for many animals.

TEACHER: And perhaps the beginning of life or youth for people too?

CLAIRE: The carriage at the end is pushed by an angel.

STUART: No, it's the little girl after . . .

TEACHER: This page [the last picture in the book] causes a lot of discussion. People don't know what to make of it.

GWILYM: She has grown up, she has learned to play on her own and be independent. In every other picture she is playing or doing something with Granpa, in this case she's alone.

TEACHER: Perhaps life goes on. Do you think Granpa has died?

LEE: He has got his medicine out on the table and then next page it is gone.

TEACHER: What do you think of that part? All the signs are he has got a cold – that's Vaseline, a thermometer.

STUART: It's getting cold in the winter, perhaps he catches pneumonia – and died. And they have been playing in the snow.

CATHERINE: He could be in hospital.

STUART: She looks very sad, because his chair is empty.

CATHERINE: I don't like to think of such a lovely character dying. I don't like to read books where he dies so in my mind I tell myself a different story.

TEACHER: Do you like the book?

MARTIN: I like 'worms go to heaven'. It's thoughtful.

LEE: I like 'can we stay here forever?' That's what I used to say at the beach.
(Disturbance.)

TEACHER: What do you think the book is about?

CANDY: I think it's about a child's relationship with her grandfather. I think it's a very good book – if that's what it's about. It's very truthful from a child's point of view. But it's also about death, and children need that.

STUART: How people get old, about life.

TEACHER: Yes, definitely, that's very good. I think that too. What would you tell a friend about it? What about the language in the book?

CANDY: It's very clever. It's just how children say things and what children do.

JESSICA: It's sad – it sounds boring – you have to read it, then you realize and think it's great.

TEACHER: Do the pictures add meaning to the story?

CANDY: Yes. For example, the [empty] chair is most important. That is what the story is about really. It's the pictures that tell you what they are doing and where they are and sometimes other things like Granpa's old games, and the words just tell you a tiny bit of what else is going on.

(From an unpublished dissertation, *Working with John Burningham* by Susan Jayne Lamacq, 1990, in Westminster College library, Oxford, pages 80-1)

You'll agree, I think, that these children are behaving, or learning to behave, as critics of the kind Auden wanted.

In preparation for the coming chapters, please review the extract, telling yourself what the young teacher did well and how she might have improved her part in the conversation. Did her questions lead the children the way she wanted them to go? Did they suggest the answers she wanted? Or did she enable the children to say what they wanted to say? Does she miss opportunities to help children express their thoughts?

For example, take the moment when she asks 'What would you tell a friend about it? What about the language in the book?' Might it have been better to separate two such large questions, giving the children a chance to answer one at a time, or was she leaving options open, implying that the children might actually prefer to talk about something they thought of greater importance? (Of course, the teacher's meaning would depend a lot on her tone of voice, and paralinguistic and non-verbal behaviour. Transcripts can't communicate these, which is why learning to teach from the printed word is so inadequate and why working as an apprentice is so important.)

SOME CONCLUSIONS

I could go on giving examples, building up evidence in support of the view that all children are (or can be) critics, at least within the bounds set by Auden:

1. There is no doubt that children introduce each other to unfamiliar authors. Anyone who has observed children browsing through a wide selection of books knows this. And we also know that children introduce adults to authors too.

2. All of us in our study group had experienced occasions when some children convinced others that they had undervalued a book. By chance on the very evening when we discussed this point, Anna Collins handed me some writing by her nine- and ten-year-olds after a discussion of *Sun Horse, Moon Horse* by Rosemary Sutcliff. 'I didn't really like the book or understand it until we had our talk. It made me understand a lot more,' one girl wrote, as if in answer to our question. 'I think,' wrote another, 'all the comments the people made made the story come alive for me, because I didn't get it at first.' And, as before, we adults found ourselves remembering when our own opinions were revised by children's comments.

3. At first we were tentative about whether children could show each other 'relations between different ages and cultures'. Certainly, it is usually adults who do this for children, because they know more. But was this simply because they don't ever suggest children do this for themselves?

   The question 'What should the teacher do?' raised itself again, as it did frequently during our study.

4. This relates to (2), and we had plenty of evidence to show that children give 'readings' which increase their own, and our adult, understanding of books.

5. Asking ourselves why it is always the adult who 'throws light on artistic "Making" ' for children, we could see no reason why, sometimes at least, children should not explore this for themselves in the work of writers who particularly interest them.

   For my part, having often visited classrooms as an author, I can testify to the keen interest children show in how a book was 'made', using working papers from first tentative idea to finished volume. Frequently, in return, they tell me about their experience of writing, comparing it with mine.

   That they can throw light on the process to their own benefit I personally have no doubt. It is all – again – a question of what the teacher asks of the children and how various in kind is the children's own experience of different forms of writing.

6. Here is six-year-old Paula throwing light on 'the relation of art to life' as she brings her world to the text of Charles Keeping's *Charley, Charlotte and the Golden Canary* in a piece of writing from *A Book All About Books* referred to earlier, and this time in an unedited quotation:

> Charley and Charlotte were good friends and they played together by the bird stall I was sad when Charlotte went to the high block of flats and Charlottes mother no longer let Charlotte play I like playing with my friends and when I can't I feel upset. I feel sad because Jessica is going to leave our school and I will miss her very much.

And her classmate Katie on *Railway Passage*:

> Mrs Hopes read us a book about people who lived in the train cottages Here is my oppinion of it. there were two people were kind at the beginning of the book and they were still kind at the end. The money didnt make much difference to the people the miserable people got even more miserable after they had won the money. I think if I won a lot of money I would by new clothes but I don't think I would be happy because I would war them and they would get worn out and I would be miserable again.

We could all recount occasions in booktalk when children moved from a discussion of the story to comment on related topics: money, family life, scientific information, moral and ethical problems, and so on. For example, when we studied children's responses to Philippa Pearce's *The Battle of Bubble and Squeak* we found that there was usually a great deal of talk about the morality of Alice Sparrow's attempt to get rid of the gerbils by putting them out for the garbage men to take away. Often this extended into a discussion of the rights of animals, and, by further extension (and bringing the talk back to the text), the rights of children as against parents and the rights of parents as against children. There was also talk about the natural history of gerbils as well as numerous anecdotes about family arrangements and tensions, comparing Philippa Pearce's fictional family with their own real ones.

Indeed, some teachers use literature solely for this purpose, so easily do children engage in it. For many years *My Mate Shofiq* by Jan Needle was all too often read with ten- to thirteen-year-olds mainly because it deals controversially with racial prejudice and so stimulated heated talk about that subject. In other words, it was used like a social worker's case study or a documentary piece of journalism, merely as a starting point for investigation of a social issue.

A similar example. A class of ten-year-olds was talking about Emma Smith's *No Way of Telling*. They were attracted by the idea of being snowbound, as the girl protagonist is. Soon they began telling equally exciting incidents from their own lives; and then went on to all sorts of holiday anecdotes, from which they wandered into a discussion of what they would do if there were no school and they could do as they liked all day. They found this very entertaining. Afterwards, their teacher was pleased because she felt they had talked well and that this in itself was valuable. Maybe so, but their talk was not booktalk, not discussion focused on interpretation of a text and discovering meaning. Emma Smith's novel and their reading of it had very little to do with what they were talking about.

Of course every work of literature involves subject matter, but quite as importantly it is a linguistic event, a metaphoric construct, a 'made' object which creates, Susanne Langer taught us to say, 'the illusion of a life in the mode of a virtual past'. 'What texts teach,' Margaret Meek reminds us, 'is a process of discovery for readers, not a programme of instruction for teachers.' The French critic Roland Barthes emphasizes a truth that content-minded teachers prefer to ignore: '"What takes place" in narrative is, from the referential (reality) point of view, literally nothing; "what happens" is language alone, the unceasing celebration of its coming.'

Surely it is this passionate adventure with language we want for our children before all else. We therefore help them explore literature as its own story, and the story of literature is discovered in the story of our own and others' reading of it. Literature is what one ten-year-old boy called 'a kind of magic that happens in our heads', and our reading is a construct of the language we use in telling ourselves about it.

Here – to take an example from the other end of the education system – is Chris Bucco, a nineteen-year-old undergraduate, telling the story of her reading of a book that some people of all ages find 'difficult', Maurice Sendak's picture book *Outside Over There*. Using what she had learned from the 'Tell me' approach she decided simply to record what happened to her as she read the book. It is a kind of reading-narrative everyone of school age and after can tell.

> *Outside Over There*, Maurice Sendak, Bodley Head. Upon looking over the cover of this book, my first impression was that Maurice Sendak was going to take the reader into a dreamland, a fantasy world outside of real, everyday existence, and that the girl and the baby illustrated were to lead us on this venture. Then came the first few pages (before the written story is introduced) with the girl and the baby accompanied by giant sunflowers, a fence (marking the boundary between 'Here' and 'Over there'?), and little goblins in dark robes with human hands and feet. At this point I realized that these creatures would play a significant part in the story and thought the story might be similar to *Where the Wild Things Are*.
>
> The story begins – I slowly read it through and while a bit overwhelmed and confused after my first reading, I am intrigued as I know there has to be some important message(s) underlying the story. Well, a few things struck me as being salient and significant features of the story while I was trying to decipher it. One was the lack of consistency in the rhythm of the wording. The words start in iambic pentameter, 'When Pa-pa was a-way at sea', but the rhythm is quickly broken. Later, rhythm returns and disappears intermittently. Other inconsistencies are found in the pictures – in the background window the situation constantly changes from a boat on the sea to a boat sinking to goblins stealing the baby sister, etc. It seems difficult to find a clear-cut dependable pattern – constant change (could this be an important theme?).
>
> In searching for hints of consistency, I found in the pictures the recurring appearance of the 'growing' sunflower plants and of the boat (Papa – memory of Papa and/or of his words?), as well as of the fearful goblins.
>
> Well, after reading the book about 5 or 6 times, I began making some guesses at the message being told (in a very

selective manner). I thought maybe the author is depicting the growth of Ida – showing us her increasing ability to handle responsibility, to be tolerant of her baby sister even when she displayed her 'goblin' side (as opposed to her happy side where she croons and claps 'as a baby should') and her ability to take care of her sister and her family (as this change into an 'adult' mode of responsibility may have been thrust upon her by the death of her father [or his absence], by the arrival of her baby sister, or by the course of time – a combination of these possibilities also seems highly plausible).

In trying to discover an underlying theme in this book, I became more intrigued and more fond of the story the more I scrutinized it and the more the ideas 'seemed' to fall into place somewhat. Consequently, I ended up with a very good impression of *Outside Over There* where I, myself as the reader, am concerned.

Judged by Auden's outline, then, we can safely say that children are able to be critics. Children know a lot about the world in which they live. The teacher has to discover how to invite that knowledge into the discussion – then add to it, or modify it according to what she knows. And it is worth emphasizing these points:

1. Children of all ages are as various in their reading of a book as are adults. In any group some will highlight one feature, some another. And though adults who have worked a lot with children can make intelligent guesses about the features that will be most attractive or rewarding, no one ever gets it completely right. On the contrary, any teaching that enables children in the honest reporting of their responses usually gives the teacher a surprise.

2. We often underestimate the reading and critical capabilities of children. Teachers especially have been trained to assume that 'stages of development' are common to all children of roughly the same age, and to accept that children cannot distinguish between 'the real' of everyday

life and 'the fictional', or the literal and the metaphoric, or the ludic role of story (when we're 'playing at life') and the irreversibly consequential finality of 'actually doing it'. Only at best crudely true, it is wiser, at least where booktalk is concerned, to act on the assumption that children are potentially all that we are ourselves, and that in telling their own stories and their reading of other people's stories they 'talk themselves into being'. In telling their readings they activate their potentialities, but only when that reading is truly their own and is co-operatively shared, and is not someone else's reading imposed upon them.

3. In any group of children, no matter what their supposed cleverness or lack of cleverness, we find that if they begin by sharing their most obvious observations they soon accumulate a body of understanding that reveals the heart of a text and its meaning(s) for them all.

   Furthermore, even when quite complicated or abstract ideas are approached this way (through story images and talked-out interpretations) there is little that children cannot grasp. In this activity there is a balance to be found between respect for the rights of the individual as a reader and talker and the corporately composed reading of the group – the community text which is always more complex and insightful than any one individual reading can ever be.

This balance in booktalk between the individual and the community seems to me a metaphor of the truly egalitarian and democratic society. Nor is the metaphor less telling when applied to adults practising booktalk among ourselves.

24

Honourably Reportable

In helping children talk well about their reading it is essential, for children and adults alike, to agree that everything is honourably reportable.

What does this mean?

Because all too many children know that their responses are often dismissed as 'wrong', 'irrelevant', 'silly', 'not helpful', 'childish' (and worse), they learn to keep their thoughts to themselves. Dismissing what children 'really think' leads to their disaffection from school-based reading. Or they play the game 'Guess what's in teacher's head': they report as their own the kind of responses they sense the teacher wants to hear. This reduces literary study to a kind of multiple-choice comprehension exercise with the teacher as the only person in the room whose observations about a text are acceptable. To be praised or given credit, everyone else must pretend to have understood the book in the same way the teacher has. As a result pupils learn to distrust their own experience of a text and, because they become skilled at saying things they have not thought and felt, they are corrupted by deceit.

The main point of the 'Tell me' approach is that we truly want to hear about the reader's experience – enjoyment or lack of it, thoughts, feelings, memories, and whatever else the reader wishes to report. For this to happen, the reader must trust that the teacher really wants an honest reaction and that therefore everything can be 'honourably reported' without risk of denial, belittlement or rejection. A reader can say 'This is the worst book

I have ever read' and know the remark will not be treated as unworthy of attention.

On the contrary, what everyone seeks at the start of a 'Tell me' conversation is a glimpse of the text, that 'first book', experienced by each reader on his/her own. And out of these 'first books' shared by the members of the group is created the larger text, the book constructed by our talk together, the one belonging to us all.

Both texts are achieved in the same way. Wolfgang Iser describes the process in Chapter 11 of *The Implied Reader* where this passage appears:

> As we read, we oscillate to a greater or lesser degree between the building and the breaking of illusions. In a process of trial and error, we organize and reorganize the various data offered us by the text. These are the given factors, the fixed points on which we base our 'interpretation,' trying to fit them together in the way we think the author meant them to be fitted. 'For to perceive, a beholder must create his own experience. And his creation must include relations comparable to those which the original producer underwent. They are not the same in any literal sense. But with the perceiver, as with the artist, there must be an ordering of the elements of the whole that is in form, although not in details, the same as the process of organization the creator of the work consciously experienced. Without an act of recreation the object is not perceived as a work of art.' (John Dewey, *Art as Experience*, New York, 1958, page 54)
>
> The act of recreation is not a smooth or continuous process, but one which, in its essence, relies on interruptions of the flow to render it efficacious. We look forward, we look back, we decide, we change our decisions, we form expectations, we are shocked by their nonfulfillment, we question, we muse, we accept, we reject; this is the dynamic process of recreation. This process is steered by two main structural components within the text: first, a repertoire of familiar literary patterns and recurrent literary themes, together with allusions to familiar social and historical contexts; second, techniques or strategies used to set the familiar against the unfamiliar.

If we look back at the conversation recorded by Susan Lamacq on pages 122-125 we'll see some of this in action. In a 'process of trial and error', the children look forward and back in the story, form expectations, question (the ending) and muse (on what the ending might mean), accept and reject. They tell each other about familiar literary patterns (the symbolic use of the seasons, the meaning of an empty chair), and bring their world to the world of the text by alluding to 'familiar social contexts' (how people get old, how children think).

As for Dewey's note about 'the perceiver' ordering 'the elements of the whole' in a 'process of organization the creator of the work consciously experienced', a child might put it all more simply. When Steve Bicknell asked a class of seven-year-olds how they felt after talking about a book in the 'Tell me' way, Wayne replied, 'You feel like you've had another story or the story over again.'

Booktalk, I'm suggesting, should follow 'the dynamic process of recreation' Iser describes. Teachers need a repertoire of questions that assist readers in speaking out their reading. And readers must feel secure and significant when telling the story of their reading. They must know that nothing they say will be misused or turned against them, that they will be listened to and respected – and not just by the teacher, but by everyone else in the group as well. They must know that everything they want to tell is honourably reportable.

25

WHY 'TELL ME'?

On the whole it is easier to put children off talking than it is to get them started. And one of the most offputting words is the interrogative 'why?'

Early in our 'Tell me' work we learned to ban 'why?' from our teacherly vocabulary. 'I liked this book a lot,' a child would say, the teacher would reply, 'Did you? Why?' and the answer would very often be a sigh or a look of pain or shrugged shoulders or a puzzled frown: certainly a visible loss of enthusiasm.

What's the trouble with 'why'?

Most obviously, it too often sounds aggressive, threatening, oppositional, examinational.

But there are equally valid objections. First, it is a catch-all question, too big to answer all at once. No one can explain in a couple of sentences why he's liked or disliked a book. That's the reason children use shorthand catch-all words in reply: it was exciting, it was fun; it was boring, it was dull.

Second, the question 'why?' gives you no help. To talk well about a book you have to start somewhere, you have to highlight a detail you can explain easily. In trying to help people talk well, the teacher's opening questions need to give them a starting point. As we've seen, the most obvious place to begin is by asking readers to talk about details they particularly liked or disliked.

TELL ME . . .

How to avoid asking 'why?' The solution, when at last we hit upon it, was not only simple but proved a turning point, for it gave us a new style. We arrived at it by searching for what we thought of as 'a conversational glottal stop'. We meant an opening word or phrase that would prevent us asking 'why?' straight out, would give us time for thought, and would provide a broadly useful start to more subtle questions.

The phrase we found was 'Tell me'.

It seems obvious now, since it has become the name for our approach, but it wasn't at the time. The qualities we liked about 'Tell me . . .' are that it suggests a desire for collaboration, indicating that the teacher really does want to know what the reader thinks, and that it anticipates conversational dialogue rather than an interrogation.

26

Meaning...?

Asking 'why?' isn't the only offputting opening in old-fashioned teacherly interrogation. So is the question 'What do you think that means?' Just as bad are variations like: 'What was it really about?' and 'What do you think the author is trying to say?'

An understanding of meaning isn't arrived at straightaway and all at once. It is discovered, negotiated, made, arrived at organically as more specific and practical questions (see 172-182) are discussed. We tease away at the problem, separating out the bits we can cope with, and talk about those. Then by sharing the bits each of us can cope with, we gradually put together an understanding that tells us something significant about the whole text.

In order to enable this to happen, the teacher must ask the kind of questions that help the readers discover and share their understanding of the bits that seem clear to them. Now and then, like a chairperson in any discussion, the enabling adult will summarize what the group seems to be saying so that they can reconsider and shift the focus of their talk if they want to.

STATING THE OBVIOUS

How often in public, and even in private conversations, have you kept quiet because you felt that what you wanted to say was obvious? How often have you heard – or said yourself to other people – 'Isn't that rather obvious?' Where do we learn that it is unnecessary, or foolish, to state the obvious? When you think about it, the only thing people can say is what is obvious to them.

It is because children think they are meant to say something they haven't thought – something that isn't obvious to them – that they are often to be seen staring at the teacher in tongue-tied bewilderment.

The truth is that in any discussion some points may be obvious to everyone but many others are not. That's why experienced participants in seminars and think-tanks begin by pooling as quickly as they can – sometimes called brainstorming – everything that seems obvious about the topic in hand. They know that finding what isn't obvious emerges out of stating what is obvious, because knowing what we have all thought or noticed, felt or understood, is the raw material out of which we construct the meanings and understandings none of us has yet arrived at – or could do on our own

It is by sharing what is obvious that we begin to think what none of us has thought before.

I have witnessed this happening so often as groups of people of all ages talk about a shared text, and heard it reported so often by other teachers, that I know it to be one of the most exciting aspects of booktalk.

So the teacher encourages readers to start with what is obvious: to say what they think they know about a text in order to discover what they didn't know they knew. Which in turn leads them to new understandings previously unavailable to any of them.

TEACHER HOLD BACK

In an early booktalk session with older children I heard a pupil ask the teacher with some exasperation, 'But what is it you want me to say?' It was a plea from someone who had come to believe that what the learner does is repeat what the teacher herself thinks because that is what the teacher wants to hear. This teacher hadn't revealed what she thought so the pupil felt confused, threatened, anxious.

Most learners of any age tend to want to please the teacher. And they often assume that the teacher 'knows better' than they do, that the teacher has the monopoly of correct information. Of course, when it comes to the reading of a text, the truth is that the reader will always 'know better' than the teacher what has happened to him/her – what was liked and not liked, what was puzzling and what seemed understandable – because this has gone on inside the reader's head, and is hidden from the teacher until the reader reveals it. The reader alone 'knows the answers'. That is why with 'Tell me' we begin by sharing what each of us 'knows' so that we can build up a 'knowing' composed of our various understandings.

Again, the teacher's role is like that of a chairperson. We all know that if a chairperson wants to influence a committee she states her own views first and then asks the others for theirs. If she genuinely wants the committee's views, however, she holds back, and sums up what the others have said, before she offers her own. The discussion may then start again but it is based on a more open and honest attempt to achieve a decision all the committee members have a chance to shape.

The same goes for booktalk. The teacher doesn't offer her reading of a text until late in the discussion so that hers doesn't become the privileged point of view, or the one that determines the agenda – the one that highlights the topics for discussion. (How the booktalk agenda is established without the teacher doing it – how highlighting takes place – is explained on 165-169.)

Until the pupils have confidence in themselves as readers, are confident in talking to each other about the story of their reading because they know that 'everything is honourably reportable', the teacher holds back the story of her own reading until everyone else has had their say.

Sometimes children will ask the teacher what she thinks. Answers should not be dismissive but should encourage the readers to continue:

- 'I'll tell you in a minute. Just for now, I'd like to hear what you want to say.'

- 'I was going to do that, but James said something that interested me and I'd just like to hear a bit more from him while I remember.'

- 'Be glad to tell you, if nobody else wants to say anything. You wanted to, I think, Sarah.'

- 'Well, yes, but there was something that puzzled me that I'd like you to tell me about first . . . [next 'Tell me' question is posed].'

Constantly, the teacher takes the readers back into the text and the aspects of reading it that interest them individually and as a group.

Just as pupils need to feel confident that everything is honourably reportable, so the teacher needs to feel confident that she can handle what is said – that she will 'know what to do with it', and what questions then to ask. Teachers at the beginning of their 'Tell me' work often feel worried about this. The key to confidence is knowing the book very well before talking with pupils about it.

The better you know the book, the more you'll be able to concentrate on what the children are saying, and the better you'll be at knowing which of the 'general' and 'special' questions to ask.

Another teacher's worry is about 'not knowing' the answers to the questions: not understanding everything in the book herself. A shift in thinking has to take place, involving a recognition that the teacher can ask questions to which she doesn't know the answer, and can honourably report to the children that she doesn't but that we're going to 'try it out' to see whether it helps.

The questions suggested in the Framework (pages 172-182) are a guide. As experience builds up, and the teacher realizes that the thing to do is trust the book and trust the reading group's co-operatively pooled responses, the more confidence will grow.

And remember: never try to exhaust either the book or the readers. Leave something for another time. Leave some questions unresolved. Leave the children wanting more: more of the book, more talk about it. And never be afraid to bring the discussion to an end sooner than you intended, if the book has proved a poor choice or the children don't have much to say about it. It isn't a failure if this happens, but a success: children will respect you for it and be all the readier to try again with another book another day. Even doing something as simple as this can raise your confidence and the children's confidence in you, a grown-up they can trust to be honest and to do well by them.

27

How Do You Know That?

A class of older primary school children were talking to their teacher, our colleague Mary Sutcliffe, about *The Stone Book* by Alan Garner. Towards the end of the session Mark said, 'When I first heard it and when I read it to myself I didn't really like it much, but now that I've got more clues, you know, I know what it's like and I understand it more. I like it better now.' (From an unpublished dissertation, 'Children's Responses to Books' by Mary Sutcliffe, June 1987)

Mark is telling us what every skilled reader knows: finding clues that help you discover the kind of story you are reading leads to better understanding, and understanding leads to pleasure. Clues were found by the children saying what they had noticed (what was obvious to them), stating their difficulties (puzzles), and then sharing their explanations of the difficulties by using the clues.

Here it is in action. The class is talking about the moment in *The Stone Book* when the child-protagonist Mary is alone in the underground cavern, where she has seen the marks on the walls (a depiction of a bull, an arrowhead shape and the outline of a small hand) and the 'crowd' of footsteps imprinted on the floor, which is formed of an impervious red clay called Tough Tom. (The commentary in italics between square brackets is mine.)

> SALLY: What I don't get is how could his [*the father's*] mark [*an arrowhead shape*] be there on the wall when he hadn't done it? [*Puzzle stated.*]

TEACHER: Does anybody understand that?
[*Explanations invited.*]

CLAIRE: Does it run through their generations to his grandfather, and his grandfather – they were all stonemasons? [*Explanation based on a hypothesis which the text neither confirms nor denies; only Mary's father is described as a stonemason.*]

ANDREW: Yes, his family's got a special mark. [*Supportive remark based on the same supposition.*]

TEACHER: The rest of the family had the same mark as him? [*Clarification invited.*]

MARK: Do you mean it was like his father and his father's father – their marks, like his arrow was his mark? Do you think that the bull and the hand were their special marks like the arrow was his mark? [*Probing. He probably isn't sure and may have sensed there is something amiss with the explanation. He is really asking 'How do you know that?'*]

Eventually Nancy said:

NANCY: Do you think it could be like a cave-painting, and they found it? Is that another story in the stone? [*Proposing another explanation (in fact, the most likely one). Clearly, the teacher feels the class need to look carefully at the text if they are to find the answer to the question so, using Nancy's question as the reason . . .*]

I recapped at this point on the stories so far from the stone – how the stone came to be there, the ridges and furrows, the bull and the patterns inside the stone cut by Father. [*These 'stories' reflect different aspects of Father's dissatisfaction with the fundamentalist account of creation.*]

Then back to the hand, referring to the text, and who might have drawn the hand – Mary's ancestors, the cavemen? At this point someone mentioned the footprints again and there was agreement that this was a difficult part to understand. [*Re-reading has focused the children's attention on – has highlighted – another problem: how the myriad footprints got there.*]

Reading from the book again was necessary – this time the section about the arrow, the bull and the hand to reinforce the discussion we'd had, and then on to Mary's discovery of the footprints.

TEACHER: Are there any clues there then, listening to it again?

Mark suggested that the prints of the bare feet were from long ago, and the shoe prints those of the father's ancestors. [*He's bringing his knowledge of the world-as-it-is to the world of the text. People 'long ago' didn't wear shoes, but many of Mary's more recent ancestors would have done.*]

There was general agreement.

ZENA: I think I get it now.

NANCY: Well I don't see why she thought she was in a crowd just because there were footprints. [*An inexperienced or inattentive teacher might dismiss this remark or attempt an explanation herself. A group of children who had not learned to respect each other and to treat each other's remarks as 'honourably reportable' might make fun of it, or be impatient, or ignore it. None of this happens. Instead the teacher makes a neutral comment that invites the others to help Nancy . . .*]

TEACHER: I see.

NANCY: When she said she was in a crowd as real as she was ... [*Because her remark wasn't dismissed, she feels able to try and clarify her difficulty. However, an interruption cuts her off at a crucial moment . . .*]

MARK: I don't get that. [*The teacher has an option. She could invite Nancy to finish what she was trying to say in the hope that in doing so she will discover she knows the answer to her own question (I think I'd have preferred to do this). Or she can allow the conversation to take its 'natural' course and see what happens, which is what she did.*]

TEACHER: You don't understand that. Anybody else got any ideas about that? [*Quoting the text*:] 'The Tough Tom was crowded . . . Mary was in a crowd that could never have been.' Why could it never have been a crowd?

MARK: 'Cos they didn't live there together. [*Reasoning based on his earlier remark . . .*]

ANDREW: They couldn't have all come together.

ZENA: At first when she [*Mary*] looked at the bull and the mark she thought she was alone and she thought it was a secret place, and when she looked at the footprints, she thought that she wasn't the only one that had been there. [*Mark and Andrew's resolutions of the difficulty are partly based on their knowledge of the 'real' world. Zena's is based more on the logic of the narrative itself. The teacher now wants to be sure everybody has understood the key point.*]

TEACHER: So what could give this feeling that she was in the crowd, because that's what Nancy is puzzled about?

MARK: Is it because the footprints have sort of been preserved down there?

Some discussion here about how they could have been preserved . . .

TEACHER: So what is it then that makes her feel she's in a crowd? Zena started to think of something, didn't you, Zena?

ZENA: Well, it was probably because the footprints were so fresh that she probably thinks that there's been . . . a minute ago there's been some people down there. [*This must have been enough to satisfy everybody, or perhaps they had had enough of this problem for now. (See page 154 on driving discussions into the ground.) So . . .*]

We then moved on to other puzzles in the book.

This discussion took place when Mary Sutcliffe was still at an early stage of using the 'Tell me' approach. Even though she was already a skilled and experienced teacher, she never actually asks the key question that lies behind all her comments and questions to the children: 'How do you know that?' The discussion would have been helped if she had.

If booktalk is to take us beyond statements of the obvious, to reach thoughtful interpretations and develop understanding, we need to discover what it was that caused us to think, feel, notice, remember, reason as we did. We need to think about how we know the things that occurred to us.

Sometimes, it is useful for the teacher to ask the question 'How do you know that?' See how it works in a simple example.

A class of eight-year-olds were discussing Maurice Sendak's *Where the Wild Things Are*. They were well into their discussion and enjoying it when they decided that Max dreamt that he went to the place where the wild things were. The teacher then asked, 'So how long do you think it took the story to happen?' The children puzzled over this for some time without being able to resolve the question satisfactorily. Eventually a boy said, 'It takes the time of a short sleep.' 'How do you know that?' asked the teacher. The boy replied, 'Max is sent to bed without eating anything. He goes to sleep and dreams about the wild things. When he wakes up at the end his supper is waiting for him and it's still hot. When I was sent to bed for being naughty, my mum didn't leave me there all night. She brought me something to eat and kissed me goodnight.'

Though his first answer – 'It takes the time of a short sleep' – is charming, it isn't necessarily persuasive. Only when we know how he arrives at it does it 'make sense' and sound 'right'. What he did, of course, was take the logic of the narrative – the sequence of plot – and bring his own world to the text: his own experience of being a naughty boy who is sent to bed without any supper. But he only reveals this because the teacher asked 'How do you know that?' It is a simple question, asking for evidence without suggesting where it might be found, and yet it is unthreatening enough to allow the reply 'I don't know' or 'I guessed'. (Everything is honourably reportable, even intuitive understandings and guesses for which you haven't yet worked out the reasons.)

Here is Margaret Mallett helping a group of nine-year-olds tell each other what they know and what they have discovered as a result of reading *The Sheep-Pig* by Dick King-Smith, along with information books and pamphlets about pigs. Sometimes, Mallett says,

> the act of reflection reveals a mismatch between our common-sense knowledge and what we read. I asked the children if reading the books and pamphlets had changed any of their views.
>
> STUART: . . . that pigs are very clean animals!
>
> MM: You had the impression before that they were dirty? Why do people think that?
>
> BEN: Because they roll in mud and things like that.
>
> STUART: . . . and they smell a bit.
>
> MM: . . . if they are kept indoors. Do they smell if they are kept out of doors, Wendy? [*Wendy's special experience (on a pig farm) makes her the 'expert' in the group.*]
>
> WENDY: They still smell a little bit outdoors but the little ones don't.

MM: It's in our language isn't it – this idea of 'dirty pigs'?

One of the things being learned here is that our common-sense knowledge is sometimes modified by what we read. It is this dissonance which can stimulate reflection.

MM: What does it say here that makes Stuart now say the pig is a clean animal? What does it do that makes you think it is clean?

STUART: It says they roll in the mud and then they clean themselves off and they go to the toilet in a separate place. [*Looking at the text and paraphrasing.*]

WENDY: Yes, they don't sit in the part of the field where they go to the toilet. [*Wendy brings in her firsthand knowledge appropriately.*]

MM: What I did not know was that pigs cannot sweat. Did you know that? [*This is mentioned in the text.*]

WENDY: Their skin is more dry and they haven't got as much salt in their body as us.

MM: How do you know that, Wendy?

WENDY: Because I asked the farmer about their skin and he said they do not sweat as they have less salt than us.

MM: That's interesting.

WENDY: Yes – because when you sweat salt comes out, doesn't it? [*Here the text has helped Wendy to reflect and make sense of her first-hand observations.*]

An essential point embedded in the basic question 'How do you know that?' is this: one of the things the teacher does is to make sure the readers keep on returning to the text, and their experience of reading it, in order for them to discover the source of their 'knowings'. Students quickly come to expect sympathetically phrased challenges to vague comments, and they begin to use the same challenges on each other. They recognize that each time they do this they get closer to saying what they mean.

But which texts should we ask children to read with such care? How do we choose them?

28

Selecting the Text

The Reading Circle (page 15) reminds us that everything begins with selection. Before we can talk about a book we need to have read it; before we can read a book we need to choose a book to read. And because the book we choose will contain within it the potentialities for our talk – subject matter, ideas, language and image, provocations to memory, and so on – choosing a book is a high-value activity. Those who choose are exercising power.

Think of the debate about the literary 'canon': the books thought worthy of study at university level. Think of the everlasting worry among adults about whether or not children are harmed by reading 'rubbish' and what is 'rubbish' and what isn't. It matters because we all know, whether we admit it or not, that what you read has an effect on you. (In truth, there would be little point in reading if it didn't.) The effect is not necessarily the one the writer intended or your teachers or parents hoped for – reading the Bible doesn't necessarily convert you to Christianity, reading Karl Marx's *Das Kapital* doesn't necessarily turn you into a communist, and reading Hitler's *Mein Kampf* doesn't necessarily make you anti-Semitic. But certainly there is an effect of some kind, and therefore we know it does matter what you read and who makes the choice.

The selection of books children shall 'study' in school is usually made in one of three ways:

- teacher's choice without reference to the children;
- children's choice approved by the teacher;

- required reading, the 'set book' imposed on teacher and children by some 'higher' authority: headteacher or head of department, examination system, a professionally agreed curriculum, government diktat.

Of these, the teacher's choice is the most significant here; but some general points should be kept in mind:

1. **Time**. Booktalk of the 'Tell me' kind is time-consuming. Frequently a session with nine-year-olds goes on for forty minutes or an hour. Longer, sometimes. Less usually means either that the book yielded very little – it was banal, perhaps, or too well-known and easily understood; or it was too much for the children, presenting too many difficulties that lay outside the range of their knowledge or earlier reading; or they were in the wrong mood, their minds set against the activity, and couldn't 'give themselves to it' .

Nor is age anything to go by. I've observed and heard of five-year-olds spending fifty minutes on a picture book. I've been kept going by a group of seven-year-olds for an hour and thirty minutes, reading and talking about the poems in Jill Bennett's *Roger was a Razor Fish*. Colleagues have told me of groups of ten-year-olds who needed two or three sessions of forty minutes each to get through all they wanted to say about books that have absorbed them. Until quite recently most teachers would not have thought it possible for children to concentrate for such periods of time. What makes it possible is the choice of book and the teacher's skill at maintaining the discourse.

Because so much time is needed, a high educational value is being placed on the activity itself as well as on the books chosen for discussion, which means that 'Tell me' sessions can never be a matter of everyday routine. Most upper primary classes these days are lucky if they can manage one every two or three weeks, if that. Quite obviously, the teacher must identify strong reasons for the choice of book.

2. **Context**. If you're alarmed by the implications of time, you must remember that 'Tell me' booktalk isn't an isolated activity,

it isn't the only time that children talk about what they've read, nor are these 'high value' books the only ones they talk about. 'Tell me' booktalk only works well when accompanied by less formal talk and informal gossip among children themselves and between the teacher and children in and out of class. 'Tell me' booktalk is a full-dress special activity, part of the wider everyday reading environment which supports and extends it.

3. **Honouring children's tastes**. Just as children talk best when they know that everything is honourably reportable, so children's mental 'set' – their attitude to formal talk – will be positive and favourable if they know that their tastes in reading will also be respected. This means that the teacher must display a willingness to make the children's choice part of the 'Tell me' selection.

How this is done is more a matter of the teacher's personality and experience than prescription. Some achieve it by discussing the choice with the children, some by allowing the choice to emerge from the children's enthusiasms, some by setting up committee-like pupil groups to select, say, one book per term, and so on. One teacher I know of sets a 'core' group of five books which all the children read over the course of a school year, along with a 'supplementary' list of which the children are required to read at least twenty-five during the year. I don't think it matters how it is done, so long as it is honest and understood by the children.

Clearly, there are hard questions to be tackled. Of balance, for example: what proportion of children's choice should be allowed? And what should a teacher do when children are keen to talk about a book the teacher thinks unsuitable or a waste of time? Some guiding principles:

- Be as open and honest as possible. Honour children's ability and willingness to consider why you think as you do. This will provoke discussion, itself very useful, about their and your reasons for accepting or rejecting a book, and how many of their choices should be included.

- Children expect a teacher to be decisive, and they know they are in school to learn. Once their arguments have been listened to and discussed, make a decision, explain why that is the best decision for their needs as learners, and then stick to it.

- Sometimes children can learn as much from making mistakes as from being guided by the teacher's judgement. During the first few 'Tell me' sessions it is useful to include one book chosen by the children even if it seems a wildly mistaken choice. This demonstrates the teacher's willingness to honour their taste and usually has one of two results. Either the teacher discovers from the children's talk that there is more in the book than she had thought, or the children discover that personal enthusiasm for a book doesn't necessarily mean it is a good one for concentrated formal talk – even, perhaps, that it isn't quite the book they thought it was. Besides, if the book doesn't yield much, the talk will peter out and everyone will be glad to get on with something else, so not much time will have been lost anyway. Which leads to the next point.

- Never be afraid to abandon a session if it isn't going well rather than drive the whole activity into the ground. Explain to the children why you're doing this and ask if they agree. Here is another aspect of everything being honourably reportable. (I have sometimes done this – suggested that we stop a session because I thought no one was getting much from it – only to be told by the group that they wanted to go on for a little while longer. I'd misinterpreted unresponsiveness as boredom and lack of interest when in fact all that was needed was more time for thought. I was expecting too much too soon.)

TEACHER'S CHOICE

The book selection of many teachers, for reading aloud and for classroom study, tends to be a mix of familiar favourites known from experience to be successful and newly discovered books that excite the teacher's enthusiasm so much she can't wait to try them out. No matter how well this may work in the hands of a skilled teacher, stimulating children to read what the teacher wishes, it isn't good enough. (In the hands of a weak or poorly informed teacher or one uninterested in literary reading, it can be disastrous for the children.)

The point to keep in mind is that all new reading depends on previous experience. Look at what happens when the public exam system requires a fifteen-year-old to study, let's say, a selection of poetry by Ted Hughes. If the pupil has not read or been taught much poetry, then the probability is that Hughes's poems will seem 'difficult'. If the pupil has read and been taught a lot of 'children's' poetry but only the kind that uses regular rhythms and rhymes and is comfortable and amusing in its treatment of subject matter, then Hughes's work will seem awkward, edgy, strange, unsettling, and difficult. In either case the pupil is more likely to be put off than turned on. The explanation is quite simple. The pupil's previous experience of poetry has not prepared her for this kind of writing. She doesn't know 'how to read it'.

In fact, there is nothing very difficult in Hughes's language – his choice of words, his arrangement of them. Nor is there anything particularly difficult in his poetic techniques. But he uses both language and technique densely: he concentrates a lot into a few lines. If you haven't come across anything like it before, or anything like it handled with less density, then it seems difficult, awkward, strange. You don't feel 'up to it', it daunts you, and you want to give up and go back to the familiar, to what you know better and 'enjoy more'.

The question for teachers is: What does a child need to read, what poems would prepare her for her encounter with Hughes and his kind of poetry? The same question can be applied to all reading. What should a child read in order to be 'ready' for Shakespeare by the time she is in her teens? What stories should a child read that will make it possible for her eventually to take on the great modern novelists? Is this done by reading certain poems, plays, stories – a kind of preparatory course of key texts? Or is it done some other way?

There is no single right answer to any of these questions. Too much depends on local and historic circumstances, not to mention the particularities of individual children. Every teacher has to find answers that are right for her situation. This should not be done alone but in co-operation with colleagues at school and locally. Here again talk is the key: so long as we negotiate together the answers to very difficult questions of this kind, we are protecting the interests of our children in the best way we can.

Here is an example. Towards the end of an in-service course on reading and literature in the primary school I set the course members the task of compiling lists of books they would advise every beginning teacher to have read before starting in their first job. The teachers divided into groups of five. One group was given the poetry list to compile, one picture books, one fiction for six- to nine-year-olds (to include traditional tales), one novels. The choice was limited to twenty titles each.

The poetry group had little difficulty, though couldn't do with less than twenty-three titles and regarded all of them, except three, as suitable for the complete age range, believing that poetry cannot be regarded as age-specific, except for questions of language. The picture-book group also had little difficulty but couldn't bring themselves to list less than thirty-four titles. These they arranged into 'Early encounters' moving on to 'Later encounters', because they felt there was an order in which one book would help a child to read another with more 'ease'. The fiction six-to-nine group found themselves very critical of the books published for this age – too many routine series books of a banal kind all made to look alike, they said – and after a lot of discussion finally decided on fifteen 'key' books, four 'classics', and three collections of traditional tales all headed by an introduction:

> This list is representative of the significant authors who write for this age range. It is arranged to form a natural progression within which there are at least three categories: relationships; animals; fantasy and short stories

The group making up the list of novels had the hardest time and took the longest. The problem, they said, was that there were so many books they would like a beginning teacher to know it was impossible to limit the number to twenty; and really it wasn't so much particular books that mattered as particular authors.

Their solution was to divide their list into two sections: the first of twelve books by seven authors; the second of twenty-three books by seventeen authors. Their introduction stated:

> The first section lists very important books by very important authors. The second supplements and complements them. We have sometimes given two titles, one eventually leading to the other.

So these teachers too had a view about progression, about one book, one kind of narrative, even one author preparing you for another.

Though their lists were useful to pre-service students whom I was also teaching at that time, as well as to the teachers attending the course, the greatest value was in the discussion of fundamental questions generated among the course members – which books their children should read and study and why. Whether they adopted the lists or not mattered less than that their everyday practice had been shared and scrutinized and thought about. Giving the exercise a real purpose – preparing lists for actual students in training – and focusing the fundamental questions in an unusual and practically specific way that used their own professional knowledge and hindsight – which books should a beginning teacher know, which books do you now wish you had known at the start of your career so as to be capable of enabling children well from day one? – helped the teachers come at their current everyday problems from a refreshing direction.

On another occasion a group of teachers were asked to decide what different kinds of narrative modes children should encounter by the time they left primary school, and to list books that exemplified them. Their list of narrative modes included:

- First-person narrators
- Third-person narrators
- Combinations of first and third person
- Stories written in the past tense, historic present, and combinations of tense
- Letters

- Journals / diaries
- Interior monologue
- Stories confined to dialogue and narrative action, without comment by the narrator or insight into the interior lives of the characters
- Stories told in dialogue only
- Playscript
- Stories in which words and pictures are integrally used to tell the story but are not picture books or illustrated stories
- Pictorial novels
- Comic strip
- Stories of everyday contemporary life; of fantasy; of history; of possible futures.

Which other modes would you and your colleagues add?

Their accompanying list of books tried to cover the primary age range. As time is always short they gave special emphasis to fiction that combined more than one of the narrative modes. For example, *Dear Mr Henshaw* by Beverly Cleary combines a first-person narrator in both diary and letter form and is a story of contemporary everyday life enjoyed by a wide range of readers aged from eight to eleven. *The Stone Book* by Alan Garner uses dialogue with third-person narrative in the past tense confined to action, does not discuss motive or narrate the characters' interior thoughts, is historically based (1860s), is controlled by a subtle use of image and is carefully structured, like a poem or a piece of music, as a sequence of linked 'movements' or episodes all taking place during the course of one day in the life of the protagonist, Mary.

A useful case-study of a teacher revising her work was published in an article entitled 'Irony age infants' in the *Times Educational Supplement* (23 April 1993). Esther Thomas described how she helped her nursery-aged children (four- to five-year-olds) discover the essential quality of irony:

> Having recently reviewed our provision of books . . . I knew that several were ideal starting points for children to grasp the idea of more than one level of meaning taking place at once,

and some that showed contradictory meanings . . . Surely this is an ideal starting point for grasping the idea of simultaneous meanings where they are relatively easily distinguishable

To introduce the idea of irony Esther Thomas used books like *A Walk in the Park* and *Changes* by Anthony Browne, *Our Cat Flossie* and *If at First You Do Not See* by Ruth Brown, *Time to Get Out of the Bath, Shirley* by John Burningham, *Rosie's Walk* by Pat Hutchins, *Awful Arabella* by Bill Gillham. She makes the point that children 'need encouragement to look at things and talk about what they see' and 'time to browse and talk about illustrations' before they 'form the habit of scanning pictures for alternative meanings'. Her experience demonstrates how a teacher can design a programme of enjoyable reading-and-talk that has a rationale, an underlying purpose, helping children develop as sophisticated, thoughtful literary readers. After reporting a group of seven children's booktalk while reading *Never Satisfied* by Fulvio Testa, she concluded that:

- most of the children could see or be helped to see two possible levels of meaning in the story;
- ability to decode the text for themselves was not necessary for such understanding to develop;
- neither age nor sex affected their responses;
- adults should beware of imposing their own presuppositions on children.

On the basis of this limited sample it seems nursery-aged children can see irony at its simplest level, if suitable books and sensitive booktalk are used. The enjoyment most of the children showed encourages me to believe that repeating this kind of reading activity will extend children's expectations of literature: they will come to expect a book to offer more than the obvious.

Being able to read between the lines also includes the recognition of the different possible interpretations of meaning. Children need to hear alternative versions of the same story in fiction, and, later, to be aware that different newspapers may present conflicting accounts of 'the truth', as do different historians and different scientists.

Esther Thomas's review of her work and what she was trying to achieve led her to conclusions about very young children's capabilities that earlier in her career she might not have thought possible, that certainly would have been questioned by the majority of adults working with that age group. Reviewing her work also led her to put together a coherent sequence of books intended to develop a particular aspect of her children's reading experience. We all need to do this, whatever stage of education we work in.

Try adding your own examples of 'key' books to your list of essential formal encounters; and do the same thing with a group of colleagues. Your book knowledge will be tested in this way; and you'll soon become aware of gaps you need to fill.

READING RECORDS

A related point to do with developing children's awareness. If all new reading depends on earlier reading then it is obvious that an enabling adult needs to know what a child has already read and has heard read aloud if the adult is to make informed decisions about what to offer next. We can only do this if a book-by-book record is kept of the child's reading. I deal with this in detail in Chapter 8, 'Keeping Track', in Part One, *The Reading Environment*.

In brief: the teacher's choice for booktalk should have a rationale, should not be arbitrary, should not only rely on the impulse of the moment. And it needs to be reviewed and refreshed regularly, just as your book knowledge needs to be increased all the time, which means keeping in touch both with what is being published and with other enabling adults who share your reading and your teaching strategies.

29

Reading the Text

The nature and quality of our talk about a book depends a great deal on our reading of it – how much attention we've paid, which parts bored us, which we skipped, which excited us, which made us thoughtful, which stirred strong emotions, which provoked memories of our past life and of our previous reading, which taught us things we didn't know, and so on. Clearly, then, if we are to help children talk as well as they can about a book we must think about the circumstances of their reading – where and when it will be done. *The Reading Environment* goes into these aspects of the subject in detail. Here it can be discussed under these headings:

IN-CLASS READING

Because money is always short and book funds are smaller than ever, a main problem of all shared reading in school is having enough copies of any one book, so we need to make careful decisions about which kind of shared reading suits which books. Some novels are best read privately by children outside classtime. Some books work very well when read aloud and can then be passed around for a second reading by children on their own or in pairs or threes. Poems and some short stories can be printed out (within the terms of the copyright law of course). Most schools build up a collection of sets of books that staff find regularly useful. But all old hands tell stories of stock cupboards that hide piles of sets bought over the years in fits of enthusiasm or by teachers who moved on, leaving behind expensive legacies that no one now wants to use.

OWN-TIME READING

Otherwise known as 'homework'. For most children this means that reading becomes a chore and the pleasure is lessened if not lost. Which is why the books chosen for booktalk should as often as possible emerge from the children's own enthusiasms – or at least appear to do so, for a good teacher is skilled at generating reading enthusiasms for books she wants the class to read. But teachers shouldn't be afraid now and then to require that a book be read; and with older pupils it is unavoidable because of the demands of the curriculum and the examination system. So long as there is a mix of choices, occasional requirement needn't become deadening or boring. It is unvarying and regular teacher-choice required to be read for homework that has helped make so many unwilling, disaffected readers.

REREADING

Children know the pleasures of re-reading; they constantly reread favourite books. Critics know the necessity of rereading; it's the only way to get to know a text well enough to complement it with more than superficial pastime attention. Of course, experienced readers can do more with a one-time reading than can inexperienced readers. But whatever your facility, the point remains: books that are worth bothering with at all are worth (may demand) rereading.

One Canadian teacher I know, Mary Mesheau, has a legend pinned on the wall about how reading a book for the first time is like making a new friend and rereading is like returning to an old one (a good summary of Wayne C. Booth's book *The Company We Keep*). When I visited her class of ten-year-olds the children talked to me about multilayered stories (their phrase). I explained I thought of this like the layers of soil and rock, one beneath another, in the ground beneath our feet. They explained that they thought of it like a cake with various layers of filling.

I am not suggesting that we should always require rereading for 'Tell me' booktalk, rather that we should encourage it for its own sake, confirming its value and rightness when we find children rereading a book because they want to or think it will help their studies. And I am suggesting that we should employ subtle techniques for helping children to reread as part of their booktalk activity. (I explained the importance of the question 'How do you know that?', one result of which is to guide the reader back to the text to find out what provoked the response.)

Equally, one of the benefits of well-run booktalk is that children often want to reread a book because of what other children have said about it. In other words, rereading doesn't necessarily come before the talk but after. And sometimes that leads to more talk, whether formal or informal.

Picture books, poems and short stories are more easily reread before or during the talk than are longer novels, which is one reason why many teachers resort to such texts more often for booktalk sessions. Be wary of this, otherwise some forms of narrative that children should encounter may be skimped or left out.

TIME BETWEEN READING AND TALK

Don't expect the same maturity of response after a text has been read for the first time as you get if there has been an interval between reading and talking, when the children have had a chance to mull it over. Of course the time-gap mustn't be so long that significant details are forgotten. A weekend is often just right, two weeks too long, unless the text is short and can be reread just before the talk. You can often sense, after a reading, whether or not a book should be left alone for a while. And once children are familiar with the 'Tell me' approach, they will let you know when they feel the need to think about a book or to reread it before talking. Indeed, this becomes part of the activity of telling each other about their reading.

Whether you need to pause and think, be private with the book-in-your-mind, perhaps to glance again at one passage and another: all this belongs to the experience of that particular text. In this way the time it takes becomes part of the pleasure of reading.

INFORMAL TALK BETWEEN READINGS

During the serialized reading of a book there will usually be opportunities for informal booktalk. This can be very important in sustaining interest in longer novels.

30

Highlighting

All reading begins by selecting something to read. All booktalk begins by highlighting – by selecting what to talk about.

In the teacher-dictated model of how booktalk should be conducted, it is usually the teacher who chooses the topic. If the class is studying, for example, *Macbeth* the teacher might begin by saying something like, 'Last week we thought about the influence of the three witches on Macbeth, this week I want us to think about Lady Macbeth . . .' Or if the class has read *The Eighteenth Emergency* by Betsy Byars the teacher might direct the talk onto the subject of bullying. Even if the teacher asks 'What seemed to you the most important thing about this story?' she will generally select from what is offered the topic that most interests her, or that she thinks most beneficial for the class to discuss.

There's nothing intrinsically wrong with this approach, and I am not suggesting that it should be abandoned completely; it has a place as a teaching strategy. But I suspect it pays scant regard to what has most interested or seemed significant to the student readers. It is about the readers discovering the book the teacher wants them to find rather than co-operative talk in which a community of readers makes discoveries far beyond anything they could have found on their own.

For this kind of mutually co-operative talk, the critic Wayne C. Booth coined the term 'coduction', from the Latin co ('together') and ducere ('to lead, draw out, bring, bring out'). In other words, in coductive booktalk we all, as a community of readers, co-operate to draw out of each other what we think we know about a text and our reading of it. It is this kind of co-operative talk that the 'Tell me' approach attempts to achieve. If this is to be a genuine intention on the part of the teacher, the topics selected for discussion must come from the readers as a group rather than from the teacher or indeed from any one dominant person.

How is this achieved? By a simple prelude to the discussion itself. We begin by discovering what it is that occupies our minds, out of which will emerge the first topic to be highlighted. In this way:

HIGHLIGHTING THE FIRST TOPIC FOR TALK

1. **Four Basic Questions.** The teacher, or the booktalk leader (for it need not always be a teacher), asks in turn the four basic booktalk questions: Tell me . . .

- Was there anything that you liked about this book?
- Was there anything that you disliked?
- Was there anything that puzzled you?
- Were there any patterns – any connections – that you noticed?

Readers are asked only to call out short headline-like replies, one word, if possible, and not to explain anything.

Each question is taken in turn, giving the group long enough to offer what seems obvious to them. As soon as further replies need to be thought about, the teacher moves on to the next question, though making it clear that replies to previous questions can still be added to the lists.

The readers' words should be used in making the lists. If you (the teacher/leader) are not clear, use the 'Do you mean . . . or do you mean . . . ?' technique of suggesting possibilities to clarify the confusion but then still use only the words offered by the reader.

Write the lists down; at best on the board or an overhead projector – something large enough for all the group to see. If that can't be done, or for a change, write them on a large pad. The key thing is that the lists must be recorded so that they can be referred to later. But for the best results, the readers must be able to see them for themselves.

LIKES

The way the snail came on the bottom of the pages

I liked it because I am 9 and have asthma and I have a brother who is 7. (Note: no father in family)

The thought of getting a job as a straight line drawer

Liked him telling about his own worries

The way his mum called him the dearest boy in all the world all the time

The sudden beginning

The whole book, because it was different

His sister making up a foreign country to fit the strange coin

His sister pretending to be a TV interviewer

The way he helped his sister when she had an asthma attack

The way he had of doing his own way of things

The way he worried about his wife and children in the future

`I don't usually like to read books twice, but that one I want to read myself now that you have read it to us.'

DISLIKES

The way Tim talked about his dad dying all the time

The way his sister was afraid of dying of asthma

When he was sitting on the pavement and looking at the ground all the time

The sign and the hat and expecting people to put money in it. He was begging.

Difficult to get interested at the beginning

The ending

THINGS THAT PUZZLED ME

The way it ended – neither happy nor sad. Didn't really make sense but the drawings helped

The castle on the snail. I wasn't sure what it meant

Putting sugar in the tea after an asthma attack

His mother letting him beg for money

The foreign coin

The way no one tried to mug him when he was sitting on the pavement

The way his sister made fun of him when he was on the pavement

ANY PATTERNS NOTICED

Snails

The castle on the snail

His sister's asthma attacks

His worries

The snail with the load being overtaken by the other snails

The link between the book his sister gave him, the story of his problems and the snails on the page

His father's hat.

Figure 1

LIKES

- The way the snail came on the bottom of the pages
- Getting a job as a straight - line drawer
- Tim telling about his worries
- His mum calling him dearest boy all the time
- The sudden beginning
- The whole book, because it was different
- His sister pretending to be a TV interviewer
- The way Tim helped his sister when she had an asthma attack
- Having his own way of doing things
- Worrying about his wife and children in the future

DISLIKES

- Tim talking about his dad all the time
- His sister being afraid of dying of asthma
- Tim sitting on the pavement and looking at the ground all the time
- The sign and the hat and Tim expecting people to put money in – he was begging
- Difficult to get interested at the beginning
- The ending

PUZZLES

- The way it ended
- Didn't really make sense but the drawings helped
- The castle on the snail – wasn't sure what it meant
- Putting sugar in the tea after the asthma attack
- His mother letting him beg
- The foreign coin
- Why no one tried to mug him when he was sitting on the pavement
- The way Evie made fun of Tim when he was sitting on the pavement

PATTERNS

- Snails
- The castle on the snail
- His sister's asthma attacks
- His worries
- The snail with the load being overtaken by the other snails
- The link between the book his sister gave him, the story of his problems, and the snails
- His father's hat

Figure 2

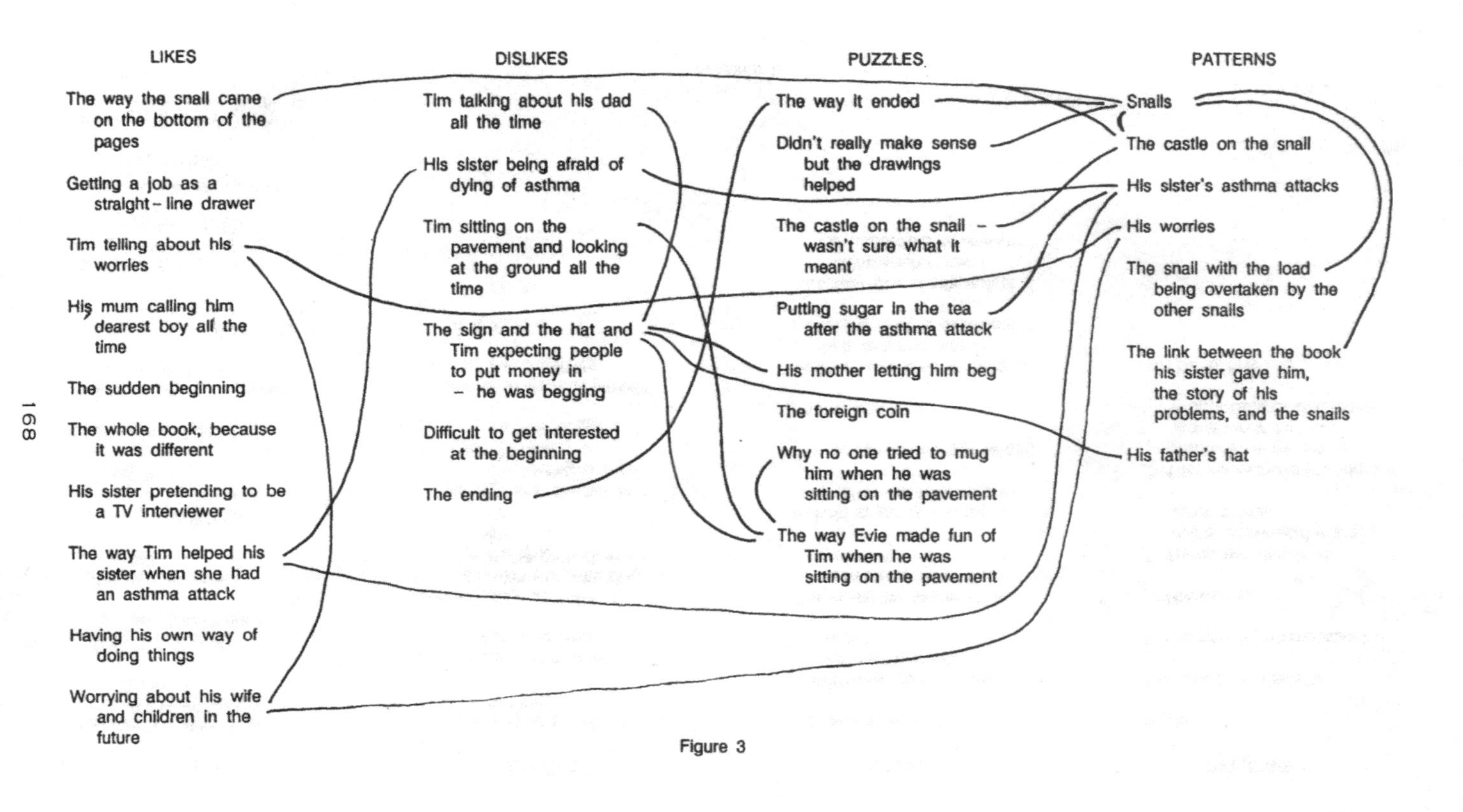
LIKES
The way the snail came on the bottom of the pages
Getting a job as a straight-line drawer
Tim telling about his worries
His mum calling him dearest boy all the time
The sudden beginning
The whole book, because it was different
His sister pretending to be a TV interviewer
The way Tim helped his sister when she had an asthma attack
Having his own way of doing things
Worrying about his wife and children in the future
DISLIKES
Tim talking about his dad all the time
His sister being afraid of dying of asthma
Tim sitting on the pavement and looking at the ground all the time
The sign and the hat and Tim expecting people to put money in – he was begging
Difficult to get interested at the beginning
The ending
PUZZLES
The way it ended
Didn't really make sense but the drawings helped
The castle on the snail – wasn't sure what it meant
Putting sugar in the tea after the asthma attack
His mother letting him beg
The foreign coin
Why no one tried to mug him when he was sitting on the pavement
The way Evie made fun of Tim when he was sitting on the pavement
PATTERNS
Snails
The castle on the snail
His sister's asthma attacks
His worries
The snail with the load being overtaken by the other snails
The link between the book his sister gave him, the story of his problems, and the snails
His father's hat

Figure 3

Let's look at an example. The book involved was *The Dearest Boy in All the World* by Ted van Lieshout; the readers were a year four class (eight-year-olds) with their teacher, Hazel Biggs, in a school in Perth, Western Australia, sometime in January 1990. There are three versions. Figure 1 (page 166) shows the answers to the four basic questions recorded in shopping-list style. Figure 2 (page 167) shows the lists presented diagrammatically, as on a chalk- or whiteboard: easier to see and to make comparisons between the various headline entries.

2. **Highlighting**. Figure 3 (page 168) shows how the agenda is decided. When the lists have been compiled, the readers are asked to identify any topic included in more than one column and/or mentioned more than once. These are joined by lines drawn to and from them. If there is any doubt about whether an entry does or doesn't refer to the linking topic the person who offered that entry is asked to decide.

When all the combinations have been joined together, we look to see which entry has most lines leading to it, and this is chosen as the first topic for discussion. If you look at Fig. 3 you'll see that the twin subjects of 'Snails' and 'The castle on the snail' are most often identified, with the business of Tim begging and using his father's hat for the money coming next.

In fact, the truth is that any one of the headlines could be taken as a starting point, because everything mentioned has been provoked by the text; any one of them, therefore, would get the talk going and could lead somewhere useful. However, by highlighting in the way suggested we ensure and demonstrate that the preoccupation of no one member of the group is privileged over anyone else's. From the process of pooling our interests has emerged a topic that interests a number of people in the group. A decision has been negotiated without anyone (and especially not the teacher) being able to exercise dominating control over the others. The result is that everyone feels better disposed to accept this as the place to begin: it feels fairer, more agreeable. Which helps create a set of mind, an attitude in the group, of genuine co-operation, of coduction.

GETTING THE TALK GOING

After the highlighting, the teacher asks each reader who suggested a linked entry to say a little more – whatever she wishes – about her headline. Begin with the likes and dislikes, move to the puzzles, and leave those who saw patterns till last – because it is the discovery of patterns, and the reasons for them, that leads to an interpretive understanding of a text or a particular aspect of it. By moving towards a discussion of recognized patterns, of connections between features in a text, we map the process of interpretation itself, and show it in action. In other words, proceeding in this way is in itself a teaching act. We're teaching children to make meaning, and at the same time showing how that is done.

Inevitably, as this talk develops, new insights will be added, comments made that are intended to be helpful but prove to be red herrings or blind alleys. Anecdotes – world-to-text – will be told, memories of other books brought into the conversation. The talk will convolute, elaborate on itself, flounder for a while (no one knowing quite what to say next: be patient, wait, it'll happen), turn back on itself, suddenly jump from one topic to another. Remember Iser (page 134).

> The act of recreation is not a smooth or continuous process . . . We look forward, we look back, we decide, we change our decisions, we form expectations, we are shocked by their nonfulfillment, we question, we muse, we accept, we reject . . .

That is what happens when we are talking well about a book. All along the teacher will do four things:

1. Keep on bringing the readers back to the text by strategies such as asking 'How do you know that?' or 'What/where is your evidence for that?'

2. Be ready to ask 'general' questions that might help develop the talk (see next chapter), and also:

3. Be ready to ask a question particular to the book in hand. By accident of habit these book-specific questions have

come to be called by students to whom I've taught the 'Tell me' approach the 'special questions' (as opposed to the basic and general questions that start the talk and develop it). They are intended to help readers find a way into the text that they haven't been able to locate for themselves. They are neutral in the sense that they do not betray the teacher's reading of the book, but they do help highlight a feature of the book that the readers haven't yet considered and which, in the teacher's judgement, they would find it useful to think about.

It is in asking the special questions that the teacher moves from being an enabler of the conversation – a kind of chairperson and facilitator – to being a teacherly participant in deciding what shall be talked about. This centrally important aspect of 'Tell me' booktalk is dealt with in the next chapter.

4. Now and then, when you judge it is appropriate, sum up what seems to have been said so that everyone has a chance to remember, to find some coherence in the talk, and eventually to reach interpretive understandings: propositions, agreements, disagreements to do with meaning. In other words, the teacher helps make sure that it is, in Wayne Booth's words, 'a kind of conversation that might get somewhere – not just a sharing of subjective opinions but a way of learning from one another . . .'

This is only one method of highlighting, an especially useful way to begin when pupils and teacher are unfamiliar with one another. After a while, as confidence and trust grow, other co-operative reader-responsive ways of setting the agenda will suggest themselves, as examples included in Chapter 32 demonstrate.

31

The Framework of 'Tell me' Questions

THE BASIC QUESTIONS

As children get used to the 'Tell me' approach, they tend not to bother with the questions about likes and dislikes but move at once to the puzzles and patterns. They have learned that talking about what has puzzled them and finding patterns in the text give them the most satisfaction. Answers to the first two questions are not abandoned altogether, however, but are woven into the talk about mysteries and connections. That is, they tell what they liked or didn't like when this will contribute directly to their understanding.

THE GENERAL QUESTIONS

These questions, which can be asked of any text, widen the scope of language and references, provide comparisons, and help by bringing into the conversation ideas, information, opinions that assist understanding.

Some of the general questions are always applicable, such as 'Have you read any other stories [books, poems, whatever] like this?' Our facility with new texts depends a great deal on our previous reading. Comparing a new text with others that seem to have similarities or contrasting features helps sort out ideas about the new one.

Some variations on the opening basic questions encourage different ways of approaching a text. Like this: 'When you first saw the book, even before you read it, what kind of book did you think it was going to be? . . . Now you've read it, is it what you expected?'

Then there are questions that help round off the talk and draw conclusions: 'What will you tell your friends about this book?' 'We've listened to each other and heard all sorts of things about this book. Were you surprised by anything someone else said?'

'How many different stories [alternatively: kinds of story] can you find in this story?' is a question that helps the discovery that any worthwhile text is multilayered, that it can mean more than one thing, that it offers different kinds of meaning. If you ask it, for example, of Philippa Pearce's novel *The Way to Sattin Shore* you're likely to be told that there is:

- a mystery-detective story about Kate's father;

- a family story to do with the relationships between Kate and her mother and grandmother and brothers;

- a story about childhood and what it is like to be Kate, who has friendships, keeps a petted cat, plays games, cooks, enjoys a day out in the snow, goes cycling, and so on;

- an adventure story centred on the ride to Sattin Shore;

- and a story about language and how it can be interesting in itself: The first few pages play with images of light and dark; the beginning takes about the same time to read aloud as the action it describes would take to happen; it is full of biblical images (the main title includes the words 'the way', which echoes 'I am the way, the truth and the life'; the first chapter title, 'The Beam of Darkness', puns on 'before you take out a mote from your brother's eye first take out the beam from your own').

The reader who made this last point helped us to find another story in the book, one based on Christian redemption, and it was only when this occurred to us that some who had been dissatisfied with the ending, because they were thinking of it in a too literal, narrowly realistic sense, saw how it could be read satisfyingly as a metaphor, a language game.

I'm reminded of Roland Barthes' words: 'To read [to listen to] a narrative is not merely to move from one word to the next, it is also to move from one level to the next.' One level of language-use to the next, one level of story-making to the next, one level of meaning to another. This is how skilled readers read; it is how we should help children to read. My experience is that they are entirely capable of it at every school age, if only the teacher understands how to enable them by providing richly made books, time to read them, time to talk about them together, and knows which questions to ask.

But it isn't only a matter of the teacher having questions ready in her head. She will also be tuned to the conversation, using questions – 'general' or 'special' – when she feels they will bring out something that is trembling on the edge of being said or help a child to articulate something only vaguely felt. The point is that the questions shouldn't be used indiscriminately when there is a lull in the conversation or when the teacher feels compelled to cover more ground.

'One of the things that makes this kind of booktalk endlessly attractive,' Lissa Paul wrote to me, 'is the way each group develops its agenda. It helps if teachers remember that – it also makes them less anxious to make sure that the same things come out every time.'

THE SPECIAL QUESTIONS

Every book possesses its own peculiarities: of language, of form, of content, and the mix of these that gives it its particular identity. In a human being we'd call this personality.

What we hope is that readers will discover these particularities for themselves as they discuss a text. And this does happen far more often than inexperienced teachers suppose. Indeed, child readers quite frequently notice significant features which the adult hasn't. On these occasions they teach the teacher.

But sometimes the group needs help. Then the teacher must ask a 'special' question, one that helps move the conversation towards discovery of the features they haven't noticed so far.

Some examples:

1. 'How long do you think it took the story to happen?' Look back at the example on pages 147-148 when the teacher asks this question of Maurice Sendak's *Where the Wild Things Are*. It is often a useful 'special' question because many stories for children make a significant, thematic use of time. Discovering how it affects the events and characters in the story reveals a lot about the underlying meaning of the text. Ask it of the picture book *Granpa* by John Burningham, the poem 'My Mother Saw a Dancing Bear' by Charles Causley, the novels *The Crane* by Reiner Zimnik, *Playing Beattie Bow* by Ruth Park, *Slake's Limbo* by Felice Holman, *I Am the Cheese* by Robert Cormier and in each case different kinds of textual 'clues' will very quickly be found.

2. 'Whose story is this?' Asked, for example, about Philippa Pearce's *The Battle of Bubble and Squeak*, nine- to eleven-year-olds find themselves discovering that the story is almost exactly shared half and half between Sid, who wants to keep the gerbils, and his mother, Alice Sparrow, who does not. This leads them to consider in a different way the social relationships hidden at the heart of the narrative.

3. 'Which character interested you the most?' is a related question. It highlights differing views among the readers about people and how they behave. I have in mind a discussion in which a group of students were telling me about the characters in *The Battle of Bubble and Squeak*. After a while a male student who hadn't yet spoken, said, 'Nobody's mentioned Bill, the stepfather. He's the character that interests me the most.' The student went on to tell us that he had a stepfather and explained, as he understood it from personal experience (world-to-text), the role of the stepfather in the story, how the story would have been different if the stepfather had been the children's birth

father, how delicate a path a stepfather has to tread between supporting the mother and yet helping the children. What he told us shifted our view of the book, made us attentive to ideas and realities we hadn't thought about: to the way it handles the assumed rights of children and of parents, the way it lets us see into the mind of Alice Sparrow when children's novels often keep the private lives of adults secret from their readers. The story seemed much deeper afterwards, fuller, richer, more valuable.

4. 'Where did the story happen?' highlights the importance of place in a story. The peculiarities of the setting of *Slake's Limbo* have both plot and symbolic significance; the story wouldn't be at all the same if it were set in, say, a hut in open country. In contrast, many of Betsy Byars's stories don't rely so much on place; most of them might equally well happen in any suburban setting. My own children's novel *The Present Takers* is set in a particular town and school but they don't have any special significance; I just happen to prefer using real-life settings for my stories. However, the companion novel *Seal Secret* is tied to its setting, and the key places – a holiday cottage on a Welsh farm, a cave on the seashore, and an uninhabited island just off shore – add symbolism to the simple plot. So asking this question of *The Present Takers* wouldn't add much to the talk, whereas asking it of *Seal Secret* would be productive.

This is the dilemma of the special questions for the teacher. The basic and general questions can be used with any text. It is easy to judge as the talk develops which are worth asking on each occasion. But not all the special questions apply to every text. Trying to answer inappropriate questions may even put off the readers altogether. The teacher needs to prepare herself beforehand, thinking out which special questions are relevant. With experience the teacher very quickly develops an understanding of which questions to ask and when to ask them. It's a skill that comes with practice.

THE FRAMEWORK

WARNING: The 'Tell me' approach is *not* a mechanical textbook programme. It is not intended that readers of any age should be given lists of questions and be required to answer them one after another either in speech or in writing.

The following list is intended solely for the teacher's own convenience and should not even be shown to students. It is provided only as an aid to memory. It is not meant to be slavishly followed. Questions should be rephrased to suit the readers involved.

The 'main' question, printed in italics, is followed by subsidiary or follow-on questions. Throughout, the word 'book' is used in place of story, poem, or whatever other more specific name applies to the text in hand.

Tell Me . . . The Basic Questions

Was there anything you liked about this book?

What especially caught your attention?
What would you have liked more of?

Was there anything you disliked?

Were there parts that bored you?
Did you skip parts? Which ones?
If you gave up, where did you stop and what stopped you?

Was there anything that puzzled you or you thought strange?

Was there anything that you'd never found in a book before?
Was there anything that took you completely by surprise?
Did you notice any apparent inconsistencies?

Were there any patterns – any connections – that you noticed?

The General Questions

When you first saw the book, even before you read it, what kind of book did you think it was going to be?

What made you think this?
Now you've read it, is it as you expected?

Have you read other books like it?
How is this one the same?
How is it different?

Have you read this book before? [If so:] Was it different this time?
Did you notice anything this time you didn't notice the first time?
Did you enjoy it more or less?
Because of what happened to you when reading it again, would you recommend other people to read it more than once, or isn't it worth it?

While you were reading, or now when you think about it, were there words or phrases or other things to do with the language that you liked? Or didn't like?
You know how, when people speak, they often use some words or phrases or talk in a way that you recognize as theirs: are some words or phrases used like that in this book?
Have you noticed anything special about the way language is used in this book?

If the writer asked you what could be improved in the book, what would you say?
[Alternatively] If you had written this book, how would you have made it better?

Has anything that happens in this book ever happened to you?
In what ways was it the same or different for you?
Which parts in the book seem to you to be most true-to-life?
Did the book make you think differently about your own similar experience?

When you were reading, did you 'see' the story happening in your imagination?
Which details – which passages – helped you 'see' it best?
Which passages stay in your mind most vividly?

How many different stories [kinds of story] can you find in this story?

Was this a book you read quickly, or slowly? In one go, or in separate sessions?

Would you like to read it again?

What will you tell your friends about this book?

What won't you tell them because it might spoil the book for them? Or might mislead them about what it is like?
Do you know people who you think would especially like it?
What would you suggest I tell other people about it that will help them decide whether they want to read it or not?
Which people would be the ones who should read it?
Older than you? Younger?
How should I give it to them? For example, should I read it aloud or tell them about it and let them read it for themselves?
Is it a good thing to talk about it after we've all read it?

We've listened to each other's thoughts and heard all sorts of things that each of us has noticed. Are you surprised by anything someone else said?

Has anyone said anything that has changed your mind in any way about this book? Or helped you understand it better?
Tell me about the things people said that struck you the most.

When you think about the book now, after all we've said, what is the most important thing about it for you?

Does anyone know anything about the writer? Or about how the story came to be written? Or where? Or when? Would you like to find out?

The Special Questions

How long did it take the story to happen?

Did we find out about the story in the order in which the events actually happened?
When you talk about things that happen to you, do you always tell your story in the order in which they happened?
Or are there sometimes reasons why you don't?
What are the reasons?

Are there parts of the story that took a long time to happen but were told about quickly or in a few words? And are there parts that happened very quickly but took a lot of space to tell about?

Were there parts that took the same time to tell as they would have taken to happen?

Where did the story happen?

Did it matter where it was set? Could it just as well have been set anywhere? Or could it have been better set somewhere else?
Did you think about the place as you were reading? Are there passages in the book that are especially about the place where the story is set? What did you like, or dislike, about them?
Was the setting interesting in itself? Would you like to know more about it?

Which character interested you the most?

Is that character the most important in the story? Or is it really about someone else?
Which character(s) didn't you like?
Did any of the characters remind you of people you know? Or remind you of characters in other books?

Was there anyone not mentioned in the story but without whom it couldn't have happened?

Can you think of any reason why s/he doesn't appear or isn't mentioned?
Would the story have been different if s/he had appeared or been mentioned?

Who was telling – who was narrating – the story? Do we know? And how do we know?

Is the story told in the first person (and if so, who is this person)? Or the third person? By someone we know about in the story or by someone we know or don't know about outside the story?

What does the person telling the story – the narrator – think or feel about the characters? Does s/he like or dislike them? How do you know?
Does the narrator approve or disapprove of the things that

happen and that the characters do? Do you approve or disapprove of them?

Think of yourself as a spectator. With whose eyes did you see the story? Did you only see what one character in the story saw, or did you see things sometimes as one character saw them, and sometimes as another, and so on?

Were you, as it were, inside the head of one of the characters, only knowing what s/he knew, or did the story take you inside a number of characters?

Did we ever get to know what the characters were thinking about? Were we ever told what they were feeling? Or was the story told all the time from outside the characters, watching what they did and hearing what they said, but never knowing what they were thinking or feeling?

When you were reading the story did you feel it was happening now? Or did you feel it was happening in the past and being remembered? Can you tell me anything in the writing that made you feel like that?

Did you feel as if everything was happening to you, as if you were one of the characters? Or did you feel as if you were an observer, watching what was happening but not part of the action?

If you were an observer, where were you watching from? Did you seem to watch from different places – sometimes, perhaps, from beside the characters, sometimes from above them as if you were in a helicopter? Can you tell me places in the book where you felt like that?

This is a long list, so let me repeat: **it is not intended that every question should be asked every time**. Nor that the selected questions should be doggedly plodded through in the order set out here.

Our experience of using the 'Tell me' approach is that after a while the Framework sinks into the back of the mind; then we don't consciously use it. We begin to listen more attentively to the questions children generate themselves – and use those as springboards.

'It makes the whole book discussion much more open-ended,' noted Jan Maxwell, 'and gives far greater scope for the development and expression of the children's own ideas and feelings.'

Anna Collins wrote, 'It gives a greater feeling of confidence. But I haven't used [the Framework] verbatim. Rather, it shapes my thoughts and points me to what I'm listening for.'

Steve Bicknell added, 'Each time we talked about a book I found I needed to refer to the Framework less and less frequently. I didn't need notes by my side. I also became aware that certain questions did not need to be put – the children started the discussions themselves, usually talking about likes, dislikes and boredom.'

32

Scenes from 'Tell me' in Action

I intended to reproduce here a full transcript of a 'Tell me' session, but observing teachers at work and listening to audiotapes made by others showed me how, as soon as teachers have accustomed themselves to it, they make the approach their own by adapting it to suit their own style and the children they work with. Some sessions begin with variations on the basic questions. Quite rightly, teachers allow the talk to follow paths suggested by the children's comments and responses; they find special questions more precisely suited to the book in hand than any of those in the Framework, and so on. In short, in experienced hands there is no standard 'Tell me' session. So instead of one full-scale session, here are scenes which provide glimpses of teachers and pupils enjoying coductive 'Tell me' booktalk.

You may now want to reread the transcript examples of sessions in action included in Chapter 23, pages 122-125, where we see a learner teacher at work, and in Chapter 27, pages 143-147, where Mary Sutcliffe helps her children talk about *The Stone Book,* and analyse them in the light of what you've since read about the approach.

BEGINNERS ALL

Eileen Langley was teaching a reception class of children aged five years to five years eight months when she first tried a 'Tell me' session. Most of the children had been with her for four months, about one third of them for a month. They were used to being gathered together in the reading corner at the start of the day and Eileen telling them nursery rhymes and reading them stories. But so far they had never been expected to talk about their reading other than informally. This is Eileen's record of her first 'Tell me' experiences.

One Monday morning I showed my class *Where the Wild Things Are* by Maurice Sendak. They were sitting happily on the carpet expecting a nursery rhyme session. When I showed the book several children got up on their knees in their eagerness to have a closer look. Several unprompted comments followed: 'A monster book', 'Look how big the monster is', 'He's too big to go in that boat'. One little boy grasped my ankle and said, 'That monster has feet just like our feet'. Someone else wondered why there was a ladder on the boat. I found it interesting that apart from Ryan, who kept a firm hold on my ankle, their attention was moving to the boat. 'Is it a story about a boat?'

I opened the book so that they could see the complete [wrap-round] cover and Emma decided that it was night in the book and the monster was asleep. As I showed them the inside title page, Philip pointed out that there was a mummy and a daddy monster. These children, having just started school, were bringing their own experiences to the book [world-to-text], and the picture that they see as a mummy and daddy monster is a very reassuring one, irrespective of the fact that it is a monster family. Another child informed me that the mummy monster was the one without the horns. The fact that the children were not frightened confirms Sendak's insight into children's minds.

The children had become quite excited but silence fell once I started reading, and they studied the pictures with avid interest. When I had finished the story several children asked to see the pictures again and I showed them, wishing that we had several copies of the book. The rumpus pages were top favourites. Lisa said that the monsters were having a disco. James said that his big brother had been to a disco and that these pictures looked like very noisy pictures.

I asked what they liked best. 'The rumpus' was constantly repeated. Kate said that she liked these words best: '. . . they roared their terrible roars and gnashed their terrible teeth and rolled their terrible eyes and showed their terrible claws'. These words have featured a lot in their language since then. When a normally very placid group were making too much noise in the Wendy house recently, I was assured that they were only having a rumpus! Neil, who is a very quiet child with a slight speech problem, volunteered that he liked Max in his private boat best.

Michelle said she was puzzled by the forest growing in Max's bedroom. We had to sidetrack here as some children obviously did not understand what Michelle meant by being puzzled. After a short discussion they appeared to have grasped the meaning. Several children decided that they were puzzled when Max went sailing in such a little boat across the ocean. Others couldn't understand why he didn't remain and continue to be king of the wild things. Alan was puzzled by the wild things because of their strange hair. James interrupted: 'They might not be true.' I asked if he thought they were true. 'No,' he replied very firmly.

TEACHER: Do you think Max is true?

JAMES: Yes, but the wild things are not.

TEACHER: How can that be?

JAMES: Max just made up the wild things.

Lisa interrupted to say that the wild things must be real as they had skin on their feet.

I decided to move on and leave these ideas to float for a while. We discussed patterns in the story. Daniel, who has a rather forceful personality and who had remarked more than once that he would like to be Max, said, 'Max's mother put Max to bed without any supper and Max put the wild things to bed without their supper.' Philip, who had been very quiet, astounded most of the children by saying, 'I don't think Max really went to where the wild things are.'

TEACHER: Where do you think he went?

PHILIP: I think Max had a dream.

JAMES (immediately): That's true, Philip. That's what I think.

A few of the children were still unsure but Philip had certainly enabled the majority to think as he did. A discussion on dreams followed, which I allowed to continue to let the children deliberate on the idea and on their own dreams. Friendly monsters appeared to feature in most dreams!

The children have requested this story on numerous occasions. I have read other Sendak stories to them but this remains their favourite. Parents have come in to check the title in order to buy the book as their child has talked about it so much at home. Other parents have come to tell me that when in the local library their child has picked this book and can read it ...

When I read a story with my class I always tell them who wrote and illustrated the book. The word illustrator fascinates these young children and they love using it. Emma asked if Maurice Sendak had written and illustrated other books. I showed her *In the Night Kitchen* and *Outside Over There*. Obviously she spread the news as after playtime I was asked to read *In the Night Kitchen*.

They listened and watched very attentively. Their faces reflected the immense pleasure they were getting from the story. They were very eager to tell me what they liked best. Alan was adamant that Mickey in the helicopter was what he liked best. Another child said, 'I also like the little helicopter which is hanging over his bed at the beginning of the story.' Others chorused that they liked when Mickey dived to the bottom of the milk. James interrupted to say he didn't like Mickey when he is out of his clothes. James is very reluctant to change his clothes for games so I was not surprised when he said this. Lisa commented that she liked lots of the words: 'Thump, dump, blump, hump, bump. I like the sounds of these words,' she said and kept repeating them.

Andrew commented that Mickey was in bed at the beginning of the story and at the end of the story.

TEACHER: Where do you think the story happened?

ANDREW: In Mickey's bedroom.

TEACHER: Does the story remind you of any other story?

LISA: *Where the Wild Things Are*.

TEACHER: Why? [!]

LISA: Max is in his bedroom before his journey and at the end of the story he is in bed.

TEACHER: Do you think all of this really happened to Mickey?

LISA: No.

TEACHER: How do you know?

LISA: Because when I watched television the ducks talked and ducks can't really talk.

TEACHER: So what do you think Mickey was doing?

LISA: He was dreaming in bed.

CHORUS: Yes, because he was in bed at the beginning of the story and at the end of the story . . .

The children were now capable, I felt, of having a longer story. I decided to read *The Elephant and the Bad Baby* by Elfrida Vipont, illustrated by Raymond Briggs . . .

The first comment when I had finished reading came from Philip. 'I thought the elephant would be too big to go into the house. He is very big beside the houses at the front of the book.'

Emma interrupted, 'I'm very puzzled by the elephant. He should be at the zoo. I saw an elephant at the zoo.'

Melanie suggested that perhaps there were patio doors on the bad baby's house. We turned to the pages where the elephant is seated at the table with everyone else, having tea. The children were fascinated and very amused by this doublespread. Ryan grasped the word doublespread and asked to see all the doublespread pictures again. The firm favourite was when the elephant sat down in the middle of the road and the bad baby fell off. The elephant was the most popular character and the bad baby did not merit any sympathy. Melanie didn't like when they all went in to tea. When I queried this she said, 'I just wanted the story to keep going rumpeta rumpeta all down the road.' The very young children were carried along by the powerful storyline and the commanding illustrations.

Vicky said there was a pattern because the elephant went rumpeta rumpeta rumpeta on every page till the elephant sat down. Lorraine said that the elephant asked the baby a question on every page and the baby always replied 'Yes' on every page till the elephant sat down. Michelle commented that there was a pattern like that in *Good-night Owl!* [by Pat Hutchins], which I had read a few days earlier. 'On nearly every page it says "And Owl tried to sleep" .' I was pleased that my five-year-old children were beginning to mention other books in the course of discussing a new book and that they offered comments at the end of each story instead of me having to prod for answers. As soon as we finish a book they volunteer their likes, dislikes, what patterns they have noticed and what puzzles them. (Incidentally, *The Elephant and the Bad Baby* triggered off a wave of good manners in my classroom. Never before had so many 'pleases' been uttered!)

CONNECTING WITH *THE CRANE*

At the start of her 'Tell me' booktalk, Jan Maxwell stuck fairly closely to the standard 'Tell me' approach, which is why I've included these extracts from the transcript of an hour-long session. The segments include samples from the beginning of the talk, then passages from the moment when straightforward reporting of likes and dislikes shifted into a phase of puzzle-sharing, and finally a section from the middle of the session when they struggled to find patterns and connections.

There were twenty-three nine-year-olds in the group. The book they talked about was *The Crane* by Reiner Zimnik. Jan set the scene in a prefatory note to the transcript:

> I read from the hardback edition, showing the children the whole book before we started and all the graphics [illustrations, facsimiles of telegrams, handwritten passages, etc.] before we had any discussion, which was not our normal practice, and the children, I felt, found this rather strange; there were occasions when I specifically had to stop them commenting and questioning. I had hoped to read the story within a complete week, a passage each day, but unfortunately we were interrupted and the reading wasn't finished until the second week.
>
> We held our discussion the day after I finished reading and we sat, uncharacteristically, on chairs, in a circle by the chalkboard. This is something I would not do again – it made the whole thing too formal and opened up a rather forbidding space between us. For my own reference I tape-recorded the discussion, but wish in retrospect that I had made notes as well – I relied too much on the recording to act as my memory. I followed the Framework by using the questions:
>
> 1. What did you first notice about the book?
>
> 2. Which parts did you like?
>
> 3. Which parts puzzled you?
>
> 4. Did you notice any patterns/links?
>
> These questions followed naturally from one another so that I omitted the questions about boring parts and parts the children did not like.
>
> The second question produced certain concrete incidents as most popular but then led to the question of the silver lion and the crane driver's dream (not linked together). These two incidents/characters had also aroused the greatest degree of

puzzlement. The crane driver's dream in particular dominated the conversation for a long time and led the children to consider the nature of the relationships between the crane driver and Lektro, and the crane driver and the eagle. Some of the children became bogged down with the idea that Lektro had changed into the eagle, others thought that Lektro's spirit had entered into the eagle. The dream was obviously a very significant event, and led quite naturally into a search for links and patterns. Here the children linked the silver lion with something good and the ravens, sharks and rider of death with something evil.

We talked for nearly an hour and could have gone on if lunchtime had not intervened. A total of fifteen children out of twenty-three made contributions, all of them thoughtful and relevant. Had we been sitting in our normal informal group I think more children would have talked.

[AC: In transcribing Jan's tape I have not noted hesitations and false starts; and sometimes the tape is indecipherable where outside noise broke through. Throughout, however, one of the things that impressed me was the clarity and assurance of the children's speech, a tribute to Jan's teaching. No child was required to talk; Jan picked out the next speaker from those indicating they were ready. (I've omitted her naming of the next speaker in order to save space.)]

JAN: I want to . . . See if you can remember, and tell me what you thought when you first saw the book.

CLARE: It looked quite good but it seems a sort of boy's book, and the pictures on the front . . . it looked interesting and when we got a little way into it I began to think, 'Oh this is a children's story'.

TIMOTHY: Well, I thought it was all about a crane and how they build it and what they used to build it and things, and so I thought it would be quite boring.

DANIEL: At the beginning it seemed like they were going to take a really long time to build the crane and then they were going to make the adventures . . . [*Indecipherable.*]

NICHOLAS: I thought it was just going to be on building the crane. [*Tracey speaks: Indecipherable.*]

RICHARD: Well, when I first saw it I thought it was going to be all about the building of the crane and all about the loading of the crane. The crane loading things into ships and how the actual place built up into a famous place.

HELEN: I thought it was going to be quite boring. [*It is generally agreed that these expectations were the ones shared by everyone.*]

JAN: Tell me about which bits you liked.

TIMOTHY: It was when he was lifting the town councillors across the river and he was shaking them about. And they all had bacon and egg for lunch.

EMMA: I liked it when they had finished the flood and the animals started to come again.

JAN: Did you? Yes. Clare.

CLARE: I'll tell you what I thought it was like at the beginning. It was quite nice, then it . . . I think the bit where I began to really get interested in it was where the crane driver actually put the splints made of fish bone in the eagle's broken wing. Then when they found out the man in the potato field and when he actually came down with a sack of potatoes. I thought that was the best bit.

PETER: I think it was quite good when the elephant had sunstroke. He was running about . . . [*laughter*] : . . . and the crane picked him up and dipped him in and out of the water to calm him down.

JAN: Yes. What a lot of different bits, aren't there . . .

So the talk proceeds, increasing in pace and enthusiasm as other speakers mention the eagle, Lektro, Lektro and the silver lion, and the little fishes swimming through holes in the shark. In talking about their expectations and about the things they liked the children had already offered cues for considering the main features of the book: its comic, surreal quality; and the formal relationships between such elements as dream and 'reality', the characters in the story and symbolically dramatic presences like the silver lion. Jan doesn't pick these up straightaway, however. She leaves them alone, till the children rediscover them later. The rediscovery begins when Timothy fastens on Nathan's mention of the little fishes swimming through the shark.

> TIMOTHY: I like it the same as Nathan because it seems a bit strange and I think that's the bit that I think makes me like the story.

In other words, it is 'strangeness', difference, the unfamiliar that Timothy and Nathan fix on as being most enjoyable – the very quality that many teachers say children shy away from and don't like.

Immediately the idea of strangeness is taken up. Jan allows this reportage to continue for five or six minutes before she asks if there were things they didn't like. Clare says she didn't like the crane driver's salary, as it wasn't fair! Timothy didn't like it when Lektro kept appearing and disappearing while talking to the crane driver (another of the dream elements). This leads to a discussion that Jan finally sums up.

> JAN: Timothy said it was unfair when Lektro kept appearing and then going away again. Clare said she thinks that was a dream, and Tracey said that she thinks it did mention something about a dream. Timothy said it couldn't have been a dream because he didn't go to sleep. What do the rest of you think?

There follows a period of hesitation. It is as if no one quite knows what to say next. An anxious or inexperienced teacher might change tack at this point, returning to more secure subjects. But Jan waits, allowing everyone time for thought, while a few comments are made of no apparent importance. Her patience is rewarded by an unidentified boy who suddenly interrupts the subdued flow:

BOY: I just realized that since Lektro died he could have been a spirit.

JAN: Mm . . . yes. Had you forgotten that he'd died?

BOY: Yes.

This remembering causes Clare, in a passage too damaged by extraneous noise for accurate transcription, to suggest that the eagle and the silver lion might also be spirits. She suggests that because the eagle appears at the time Lektro is appearing and disappearing, the eagle might be Lektro's spirit.

They talk about this, eventually returning to the text in order to establish the precise order and relationship of events. Jan reads the key passage out. They discuss it, puzzling out a resolution to the problem of the eagle's true identity. This becomes so difficult that they begin to talk again about parts they didn't like: in other words, they concentrate on difficulty, and do so by constantly referring to what the text actually says. All sorts of suggestions are made. Jan gives consideration to all of them.

A head of steam builds up that inevitably leads to a desire for some meaningful connection between these so far unconnected elements. Jan waits for this moment to arrive, which eventually it does in this way:

RICHARD: I didn't like the part where the ravens were laughing. The ravens were always cruel and they were always jealous of the crane driver.

JAN: They were, weren't they. Yes. Roger.

ROGER: This may sound silly but when they were laughing at the crane driver they might have changed into the sharks to try and knock down the crane.

JAN: That just reminded me of another question I was going to ask you, and I think that all this fits together somehow. I was going to ask you this question . . . Remember when we were doing our work about patterns, and I read you fairy stories, and we were looking for patterns in the stories? Now I was going to ask you if you can see patterns . . . or connections . . . in this book? Can you think of things that make a kind of pattern? Now, I think from what Roger has said I have just begun to see the beginning of a pattern. I think, I'm not sure, because I'm trying to work this out the same as you are. And I think I can begin to see a pattern that says . . . [*writing on the board*] . . . RAVENS . . . [*Indecipherable.*]

CHILDREN: Sharks!

JAN: [*writing*] SHARKS. Ravens and sharks ...

Jan has led them a little here. Perhaps she felt it was necessary to help them. At any rate, they quickly pick up the idea, struggle for a time with the misstep first taken by Clare's association of the eagle with Lektro's spirit, but gradually build up a pattern that groups Lektro and the eagle with good and the ravens and sharks with evil. This is tidied up and resolved in this way:

JAN: Does the silver lion make a kind of pattern?

CHILDREN: A bit!

JAN: A bit! Yes. How?

CLARE: Well, the river pirates are bad and the silver lion is good.

JAN: [*at the board*] So the silver lion fits into this bit, with Lektro and the eagle, all the good things, doesn't he? So he was good. And we've got the . . . on the bad, we've got the ravens, the sharks, and death – the figure of death – [*Overtalking*.]

JAN: Now we've got three things on each side. The ravens, the sharks and the figure of death. And here we've got Lektro and eagle and silver lion. Now, can we see a connection between any of those? I'm beginning to see things, I think. [*Pause*.]

RICHARD: Well, obviously, you could say the ravens and Lektro go together, silver lion can be maybe a spirit, and death must be a sort of spirit, so silver lion and death can go together.

JAN: That's quite interesting, because that's what I was thinking. Certainly, silver lion and death are kinds of spirit. Where the other things are real things, silver lion and the figure of death are not real, are they, somehow?

CHILDREN: No!

JAN: So they have a different sort of meaning from the others, don't they? Because death comes along when war is coming and . . . silver lion comes in more than once, doesn't he?

CHILDREN: Yes!

CLARE: So does the figure of death, because he comes along before the war but comes after.

JAN: That's right, Clare, he does. He does indeed! Silver lion comes when?

DANIEL: [*Indecipherable*.]

JAN: Yes. Let's try and think of the times when silver lion comes. He comes before the war, on the landing. Can you remember exactly when?

A BOY: Was it after the crane driver had been helping the circus people with the animals?

JAN: Yes, it was.

CHILDREN: Yes! [*They sort this out precisely, listing the lion's appearances.*]

A narrative pattern is being discovered and reconstructed. The class is within range of a recuperation of meaning, and in the final part of the session they begin sorting this out. Quite obviously, from the time Jan first mentioned the ravens it is possible to see that she has a critical direction in mind. To some extent she is setting the agenda. As she became more experienced with the approach, she learned how to hold back, allowing the children to shape the discourse much more.

Jan admired *The Crane* very much and wanted her children to enjoy it as much as she did. When this is so, it is hard for the teacher to remain neutral; and sometimes (as I believe it was in this instance) it is right for her to help the children find a line of thought that is productive. Unquestionably, I know from the results of this session, the children learned a great deal not only about this book but about how to enter a book of an unfamiliar kind, how to question it and how to enjoy its unusual tune. And, apart from anything else, one can hear on the tape the children's unflagging enthusiasm and their keenness to take part in the discussion.

AN INTIMATE DIARY OF READING IN PROGRESS

Liz Tansley usually taught infant-aged children. As a change she had one year with a class of seven- to nine-year-olds which she team-taught with a colleague who looked after a parallel set in an open-plan area. During this time Liz started practising 'Tell me'. When she began she was reading Cynthia Harnett's *The Wool-Pack* to her pupils, following it with *Sun Horse, Moon Horse* by Rosemary Sutcliff. Her booktalk sessions developed during readings of *The Eighteenth Emergency* by Betsy Byars and my novel *The Present Takers*. So far she had followed the plan of asking basic questions, establishing the highlighting agenda, and introducing special questions as she thought necessary. The children had done well and were soon used to this way of talking. Now she wanted to move on, to improvise more, give herself and her pupils a challenging text and plenty of opportunity to explore their reading of it. She chose *Slake's Limbo* by Felice Holman, a book I'd have thought perhaps better left for a year or two later but which she decided would extend them without loss of pleasure.

So that she could reflect on what she did and have a record to give to me, Liz kept a diary of each session. The result is a narrative account of a highly skilled teacher practising the art of her profession with great sensitivity and self-critical insight. Her handling of the book, the class and the 'Tell me' talk is subtle, complex and in many ways idiosyncratic. The analytic comments in square brackets are mine.

Monday March 10. For a change I have decided to read only to my own set, and we begin with *Slake's Limbo* today. I started by saying that it was an important book, which needs a lot of thinking about, and that it is one that I have enjoyed very much. I deliberately didn't say we might find a connection with what we had recently been listening to, as I had done with *The Eighteenth Emergency* in relation to *The Present Takers*.

My general demeanour was serious so the atmosphere was expectant but quiet and sober.

The only background I gave was a quick reference to [New York] subways and the [London] Underground, which most of the children at least knew about even if they had not been on it. 'Elevated' and 'wily' I remember I had to explain. No one could approach 'wily' until I brought in 'wily as a –', and then one child said 'fox'. I hope I remember to go back to this as an indicator to Slake's character and condition.

I read, in two sessions of about twenty minutes, up to the point where Slake escapes into the subway for the 'one hundred and twenty-one days'. I repeated that phrase when I stopped, closing the book (they always find that a quite dramatic gesture if you do it with deliberation), and there was a general releasing of breath. They immediately wanted to know more about this length of time and didn't turn their thoughts to how Slake would survive or the actual act of running away from home.

I then said, 'What would you do if you had had a bad day, or a horrible experience, or felt the world was against you, where would you go?' [*An invitation to bring their world to the text.*] To which they replied in unison, 'Home.' An immediate difference between themselves and Slake was appreciated by them, and this response shows that my age-group children are still very much attached to home as the haven, and the only one, which might not be the case as children get older. I'm thinking here of an adolescent who may be more inclined to share problems with peer group friends first, rather than the home.

So I already know that a bond of interest has been forged with the book, and from their facial expressions I could see that they were feeling a reaction that was mixed. They were both astounded at the predicament Slake had landed himself in, and sympathetic, tinged with awe at his daring.

When I asked why Slake had not chosen to go home, they were right on the ball concerning his distressing background. I asked for 'evidence' [*How do you know that*?] – they love this word. I think it may have to do with the fact that in the infants we often talk about being a detective when reading. They noted the 'kind of aunt', being 'slapped', the sleeping conditions, and the 'scraps' of food. The Americanisms in the language didn't get in their way at all. I'm always surprised at how little, if any, comment I get about the formal school set-up that is evident in all three books in this series of readings. It is so different from the experience they have had. School must have a kind of universal concept for them that allows them to accept any model.

Tuesday March 11. I could only give one home-base session to the story today. We read chapter two and 'On Another Track'. I simply said 'One hundred and twenty-one days' and went straight in.

I left phrases such as 'A phalanx of leaping weight on the hoof' and 'other fortuitous circumstances' in the flow of the narrative, but I gestured with my hands the flight of Slake from the gang and mimed the 'snaking' of his body through the gap into the cave.

When we turned the page and came upon 'On Another Track' I turned the book towards the children and drew their attention to the difference in typography. They noted the darker [*semi-bold sans-serif*] print and the fact that there was a title rather than a number for a chapter. I asked, rhetorically, why the book had this change, what purpose it served, and got a general 'Hmm' from the children. I wonder what they will make of this part of the structure as the story develops.

When I closed the book, I pursued a reaction to the knowledge they have acquired so far, concerning what is really happening at a deep level. I asked 'What are we being shown so far? What ideas are coming out of the book?' Silence. So I added 'Are we just finding out things that happen, or are there any important ideas that are coming into your mind?' [*What kind of story is this? How are we meant to 'read' it?*] Silence again, but accompanied by downward glances (always a sure sign that something is going on), and fingers on lips. Pushing further, I asked James if he remembered the word he used in describing *The Present Takers*. He did – the word was 'emotional'. [*The experience of previous reading being brought to the aid of interpretation of an unfamiliar text. It works, releasing new ideas.*] Once he said that, there was more thinking, and then another boy came up with the word 'sight'. I reacted with surprise and pleasure, saying I had not thought of that, and that we would follow the idea through. Right away two children came up with the reference to Willis Joe dreaming of driving sheep in Australia, and to Slake, quoting 'he walked a dreamer'. A younger child (Hannah) added the fact of Slake's short-sightedness, followed by another child saying the [*Underground*] tunnel was dark and Slake couldn't see very well in there. At this moment I thought it right to help them articulate the sense of what they were moving towards [the teacher sums up], and said it seemed we were saying that there was a connection between Slake's actual poor sight and his 'seeing' in his dreams, and that Willis Joe also was able to dream of other places and have feelings that were not to do with his job.

I then asked whether the word 'horizons' fitted in anywhere. This was beyond them so I gave an explanation of the word and said I thought the idea of Slake and Willis Joe dreaming of spaces and places with long vistas was of some importance when we knew city skyscrapers and tunnels shut out light and views, hoping I had added to their 'sight' repertoire.

It pleased and reassured me to get the response of 'sight'. I had expected the whole thing of tunnels and underground to be uppermost in their minds. I know I had read with emphasis whenever underground was in the text. Yet again the children's independence in assimilation and reaction to a text came through.

Confidence in the children's ability is a most important factor in booktalk. That is, that they will not simply regurgitate what the teacher thinks she has planted in their minds.

Thursday March 13. Home-base at the end of the day. The children were tired and I will read at the start of the day tomorrow. A quick recap, based on 'Slake knew he was in business'. The next part of the story is about the development of Slake's newspaper business [*he collects used papers left behind by passengers in the station, smooths them out and sells them again to people too rushed to call at the newspaper shop*]. Although the word crime is used, I think from the giggles the children viewed his action as naughtiness. They liked all the part about Slake making his bed out of leftover papers, appealing probably to this age group's delight in making dens and general 'pretend' environments.

Just before Slake gets back into his cave there is a sentence, 'Slake was –'; the children provided the word 'home' as I looked up.

We then came to 'On Another Track'. The book was turned towards the children and there was recognition of the same title and print as before. The surprise was at the short length, only one page. One boy, Stephen, said something like he thought the author was trying to tell us something. [*The book-as-object being used as a clue to meaning*.] I said, 'Well done' and asked if he could explain a bit more. He was struggling with an abstract thought, having gleaned a generalized idea of some of the 'thinking about books' vocabulary we are trying to build up. What was pleasing was his confidence in speaking like this within the group. [*Everything is honourably reportable*.] He is one of the youngest and had not attempted to lead a new line of thought for the group to consider before.

I said 'Something's going on in these bits' and read it. I thought this part was over their heads, so I turned the page, again turned the book round, to have them say 'Back to a number for a chapter'.

Time was late, but I decided to read quickly into the next chapter to keep the flow going after the last difficult part. But this was where the talk came. It's the passage where the two 'regular customers' are introduced. Several of the children were convinced it was reasonable to think the 'turbaned man' might be Willis Joe and that he might meet Slake again and rescue him. I reacted with less than enthusiasm but my grimaces and 'pardon?' were overruled in their excitement at thinking they were solving the problem of what happens next. I resolved that with a limp 'Well, we shall see'. When some children took my hint an argument broke out, involving such points as 'How could Willis Joe be buying a paper when he came to the station to work?', answered by 'He could buy a paper before he started work', answered by 'But this station would be part of his work', countered by 'Today could be his day off', and 'Anyway, he smiled at Slake' . I didn't think I stood much chance so I left it at that.

Thinking about what you once said about key children exerting influence within a group and shaping general responses, I know I rely on Dean, Katiana, James Bro., and Matthew from the second years, and Hannah, Tom, John from the first years.

Dean is a very mature and great reader. He always buys or borrows the books we read together. We only started this book on Monday. He was away Tuesday, so on Wednesday read up what he had missed. He informed me today that he'd borrowed this book from the public library and had got up at seven o'clock this morning and says he finished it! He is pivotal in my group and also when the two sets share a story together. He is physically big and generally able, popular, and so a model for other children, especially the boys. We all look out for when Dean murmurs 'Oh, this is a good bit'.

Friday March 14. Pages 35 to 42. Just flicking through the pages I came upon 'From then on the cave was lit', when Slake gets the lamp. Here is a perfect example of the way in which the give-and-take between teacher and children works. My mind went back to the talk about 'sight'. I had not noticed the sight and light imagery and metaphors when I read it myself. I now see the connection with the references in 'On Another Track', just preceding chapter five, to Willis Joe's soul and, by implication, Slake's, and beyond that, ours. Again, for me the links with traditional Christian imagery are strong.

We read *Slake* first thing in the morning, when the children were alert. I reminded them that we had begun chapter five and that Slake now had 'two regular customers'. I read to the end of chapter five, turning the book towards them to show them the graffiti and how it was typed, and also the use of a series of dots, as in the final sentence 'Slake's expectations for good were not great . . . were not great . . . were not . . .'

I stopped for a short time when we came to the part about Slake looking out of the carriage window 'as if there were sights to be seen on the dark concrete walls'. I sensed the children wanted to break in here, some leant forward and some started to raise their hands. They quickly connected with their 'sight' discussion yesterday and saw it in terms of dreaming. I think, hope, they are now incorporating the idea of day-dreaming as well as sleep-dreaming. I should try and establish if this is so.

When we came to the sentence 'He began to know the signs of the subway as a woodsman knows the wilderness' I deliberately called their attention to it by repeating it. I noticed Rebecca's concentration had gone, and reinforced my point by saying 'You need to listen to this bit, Rebecca, I think you'll find it important.' [*Sometimes the teacher supplies energy when the student flags.*] We quickly defined wilderness and moved on. [*The teacher helps by providing information the learner needs and doesn't have.*]

At the end of the chapter I asked 'Is there anything you want to say now?' A lot of hands went up. I then got my notebook out, suggesting it would be a good idea to note down some of our ideas, as we were going to have a talking session with the other set in the morning. More hands went up, and in the very short time we had left these are some of the comments I managed to get down:

'He sees things on walls. It's like he's dreaming.'

'The dot dot dots is like it's fading away, it's pauses, it means it carries on.' (From three children.)

I looked up here and asked 'Any important words for ideas in this chapter?'

Matthew: 'Exploration, because it connects with Willis Joe. And it's like with *The Eighteenth Emergency*, Mouse exploring to find Hammerman.'

Hannah: 'In all three stories the main character has been picked on.'

Rebecca (undoubtedly her attention had been regained because she attempted to quote): 'He knows the signs like he was a woodcutter in the wilderness.' Asked to add to that, she said 'The gang boys are like wild boys.'

Stephen was triggered by Rebecca bringing in 'wilderness' and said 'Slake's like a badger because at night he ducks into his tunnel.'

I raised my eyebrows at this and Stephen was immediately defended by another boy who said badgers do go into their tunnels at night as well as in daytime.

Neil: 'Getting food like in the wilderness.'

James Bro.: 'He's lost but not frightened.' (I thought this was a sensitive observation. James has the ability to get inside a character. It was he who said *The Present Takers* was an 'emotional book'.)

James triggered by Dean: 'The city's like wild because he has no friends.'

[*In these comments we see the use of intertextual references, a discovery of metaphoric meaning, the bringing of world to text to resolve a problem, and insight into character.*]

We had to stop there but later in the morning I had both sets together for a talking session. The other set are hearing the story from their own teacher. I said I wanted to use the board and try connecting the three books together. We hadn't done this before in quite such a definite way and there was great excitement from the children. There are over fifty when both sets are together but they never show signs of difficulty, listening well to each other and quite happy to agree with a 'yes' or a dissent with 'not really' if they don't get chosen to lead in with a response.

As usual I asked for [*single*] words, as this seems both easier for the children and also concentrates their minds on ideas rather than retelling the story, although they feel free to, and do, give a lengthy response if they wish. [*Everything is honourably reportable.*] Whatever I do put on the board I always comment on it and ask for evidence from the text [*How do you know that?*], even if only fleetingly. This allows other children, rather than only the originator, to join in and expand what is being noted. [*Cooperative pooling of ideas.]* I gave them the word victim after they had given bullying, and protector after ally, as I thought this would increase understanding of the texts. [*Teacher as informant.*]

I questioned their wanting to put ally under *Slake's Limbo*. They quite rightly came up with Willis Joe but I said I wondered if the book indeed had, as yet, given us any firm ideas that Willis Joe either could or would be some kind of friend or ally of Slake. [*Teacher returning readers to text.*] They decided a question mark be put instead.

Thinking about it now, their logic was better than mine, as they obviously sense that Slake, going on the form of the previous two books and many others already in their history, will, and must (to them) have an ally at some point. And as the book, and I, have made Willis Joe's place in it important, and so far he has been presented in an interesting, non-threatening light, the children were making a judgement based on reason and feeling and previous reading experience.

[*From this point on I don't provide further analytic glosses, hoping that by now you will be sufficiently familiar with the approach confidently to provide your own.*]

Monday March 17. Only time for a short session at morning home-base time. Much of it was taken up with whose parents were allowing their children to go on the 'Litter Blitz' later that day. As a result, we only got through the first four pages of chapter six. This took us up to the point where Slake feels threatened by the 'turbaned man' questioning him about his newspaper business. There was no time for discussion, but the children were worried about Slake.

At the very end of the day, in the last ten minutes, I was able to go back to what we had heard and to ask for comments. No sign of enthusiasm – it was hot and we were all tired, so I said perhaps we could jot down some thoughts ready for our next sharing session with the other set.

Matthew came in with: 'Where it says one hundred and twenty-one days in the subway, is it now in the story?' The question, it transpired, came from confusion with Slake's remembering of his time with his aunt, when he was accused of spending the bottle deposit money.

They were all quiet so I told them their thoughts on 'sight' had helped me with the book. Next, I said I thought ideas about sight were connected with light too, and said it was something to do with a sentence about Slake getting a light into his cave. They sat up to this challenge and almost got the sentence right, saying 'With that, Slake's cave was lit'. Then I said that if we looked at the two words, darkness and light, did they have anything to do with Slake's character and the conditions of his life? The responses:

James Bro.: 'His cave's dimly lit and so's his life.' I said 'What a good way of putting it', and asked for more explanation.

Dean: 'It's dull.'

Rebecca and Anouska: 'He's got no proper clothes or food.'

Matthew: 'He's got no proper friends, and dark is a dreary colour, and when it's light it's sort of happy.'

Dean: 'Yeah, the punishment he had.'

Katiana: 'When he's with his aunt he feels dark.'

What is interesting here is that it is older children only who took the lead in thought. My original question must have been too difficult, both in its phrasing and content. Younger and less mature children (I'm not putting both attributes together) did join in, mostly repeating 'The tunnel's dark', or 'The walls are dark' .

Perhaps unwisely, I went back to the tunnel and underground imagery. When asked 'Does the tunnel idea, the being underground, play a big part in the story?' there were pursed lips, heads to the side, and expressions of 'Not really' on their faces.

Still worrying the bone, and getting just a little exasperated, I suggested that tunnels, and cold, and no proper bed, and darkness, were not the usual things in our lives. I asked what the tunnel and subway meant to Slake, why did he choose to be there?

'Home', 'Hiding place', 'Safe house', 'He's protected'. The tone of voice these responses were delivered in suggested I really needn't have asked.

Somehow, we got to the word civilized. I had to explain it, then asked whether Slake's life was civilized in the subway. Immediately they came up with:

'Shelter', 'Friend, the cleaning lady', 'Warmth', 'He's got freedom from being hunted', 'Food', 'Cleanliness, because he washed in the clean toilets', 'He's got a job, his business', 'Water', 'He runs his own life' (from Matthew, I remember).

Katy, who had been ruminating on civilization all this time, grinned and said, 'Yes, but he doesn't clean his teeth'.

Wednesday March 19. Chapter seven, where life gets better and better for Slake, was enjoyed very much. The children smiled and laughed a lot, feeling a sense of relief for Slake, and empathizing easily with his classifying and pleasure in his collections. They loved the 'Good enough' response at the end, from the turbaned man (Slake's glasses), laughing and repeating it to themselves.

The whole section on Slake's glasses (page fifty-four) was very relevant to their thoughts on sight. I looked up and said it fitted in with our thoughts so far, and that into my head had come the name of a book I was sure they had all heard as infants and probably seen as a film on television. Lots of puzzled expressions, to which I responded with 'Think of glasses, coloured lenses that change how the world looks'. Some more thinking, and then a number of children came up with *The Wizard of Oz*. They talked about their memories of it for a few minutes before I led them back to Slake, asking if there were any connections between the two books. Lots of children said yes, but in the couple of minutes we had left I only got two comments down, and they were to do with sight:

Matthew: 'It's like Dorothy, the longer he stays, the happier he gets, he doesn't want to go.'

Stuart (one of my so-called less-able children): 'His aunt is bad like the bad witch in *The Wizard of Oz.*' This last comment raised Stuart's standing in the group enormously, and he basked in the approving murmurs and glances.

Thursday and Friday were the last days of term. Finishing study books, sorting out artwork, checking equipment, cleaning, etc., meant the atmosphere wasn't right for concentrated listening so the children agreed we should finish *Slake* at the start of next term.

Summer term, Monday April 7. Their interest had been maintained over the two-week break and we took up from where we left off, first thing this morning.

We came to the part where the lights go out on the platform and the word evolution is in the text. I asked if they knew what it meant. Many were unsure so I gave a brief explanation and they quickly caught on to the early-man aspect, with Stuart then saying 'The man, a long time ago, lived in caves'. Others agreed and I asked if this had any connection with what we knew of the book. They answered with 'Yes . . . cavemen . . . old rags . . . no proper food . . . no proper bed . . . drawings like the cavemen . . . scavengers for food.'

Page seventy-seven brought us back to Willis Joe, where the deterioration in his life, his poor motivation for his job, and his family are described. I simply asked if they had anything to say about this:

Rebecca: 'He's quarrelling with his wife and children.'

Tom: 'The wrong driving.' (One boy added 'Like a lunatic.')

James Bro.: 'He walks the long way home on purpose.'

After this I asked 'How would you describe the atmosphere in this bit?' Stuart, whose attention often wanders, was still paying close attention and was again first with a response:

Stuart: 'Tiring.'

Hannah: 'It's like a habit, his life's boring.'

James Bro.: 'He's addicted, like cigarettes.'

Tom: 'Because he's getting fed up with his life, he's getting nearer Australia again, he needs it.'

This last perceptive comment puzzled some children and we had a general talk on how dreams and ambitions, even, and perhaps especially, unfulfilled ones, are important to people.

Tuesday April 8. We read chapters thirteen and fourteen today. We looked at how little was left to read and the children were excited at the thought of the coming climax to the story.

We discussed the use of the word tomb in connection with Slake's almost self-burial in his cave, when he realizes the workmen are coming to block up the hole [in the tunnel wall]. I wondered if they would be able to make the connection with the Easter story which they had heard so much of before the holidays. They found this either too difficult or simply not relevant to their perception of the book, so I told them it was a connection I personally found interesting and left it at that.

In the final paragraph on page eighty-five, at the end of chapter thirteen, I drew their attention to the word tracks, just before Slake stumbles out into the tunnel.

The children were now in a high pitch of excitement, but before we started the next chapter, I asked for some comments:

Peter: 'Slake might die.'

Anthony: 'Their lines have crossed.'

Anouska: 'Slake's angry at the workmen.'

Katiana: 'If he doesn't wake up properly his house will be lost.'

Rebecca: 'I think Willis Joe will help him get his house back.'

Matthew: 'Slake's sort of dying and so's his cave.'

We just had time to read chapter fourteen. The children were delighted that Slake was safe, and also that Willis Joe had mentally made a recovery; as Neil said, 'Willis has stopped being a lunatic.'

Wednesday April 9. By common consent Slake had to be finished first thing this morning. Before we started we talked about how final chapters often bring together threads of the story that have seemed disconnected or puzzling, and that we would watch out for this as we read.

They didn't want to stop anywhere during the reading, and when the book was closed there was an air of disappointment, I felt. I just looked up enquiringly and Anouska said vehemently 'It's like a film with a stupid ending, you don't know what's happened.' We were all so taken aback by this I feared the children would feel the book had cheated them in a way, and wondered if I could rescue the experience for them. So I said that books have all sorts of endings and that this might be one of the kind that needs the reader to look back into the book to understand the way the ending has worked out.

They brightened up at this and there were two comments that helped them begin to come to terms with the ending:

Matthew: 'Slake wanted to leave the underground like Willis Joe wanted to leave his sheep.'

James Bro.: 'Slake escaped from the tomb and the bird escaped from Slake, it's got ideas of trapped and escaped.'

I concluded by saying that this was a book we would all need to think about and that I would get the tape recorder in so that they could have some conversations in small groups, and gather their ideas together, as well as putting their ideas in writing if they wanted to.

April 15. I now have a student working with me who has started reading *The Way to Sattin Shore* [by Philippa Pearce] to my set. We have finished the tapes and writing on *Slake*.

33

'Tell me' Games

Variations on a theme: strategies we think of as readerly games that allow the 'Tell me' approach to be enjoyed in ways that widen its scope and emphasize one aspect or another of its strengths.

THE SENTENCE GAME

The class is divided into small groups of not less than three and not more than five. Each group will have read a different book.

The members of the group begin by sharing the basic four questions. If they want it (or the teacher does), one of them is appointed chairperson and note-maker. When they have finished with the basic questions, they talk about any general and special questions they think appropriate or that the teacher has asked them to address. During this time the teacher tours the groups to keep in touch with what is happening and to help with any problems.

When the teacher judges the time right, the talk is stopped and each group member privately (no discussion allowed) writes down the one thing about their book they'd most like to say to someone who hasn't read it. Do not allow very much time for this; it shouldn't be lingered over but written under pressure. Next, the group listens to each member's sentence, after which they help each other revise their sentences to express as well as they can what they want to say. And finally they decide in which order they will read their sentences out to the whole class. In other words, they arrange their sentences into a paragraph. Again, this should be done quickly.

Now the class comes together. The teacher nominates a group to start the next part of the game, which should be fairly formally done, the group sitting in front of the class, like a panel, the whole business being slightly dramatized so that everyone senses its importance. The chosen group announces the title and author of their book and shows a copy of it. Then each sentence is read out in the agreed order. The teacher asks who in the audience already wants to read this book. After which the rest of the class question the group about their book. The group members must answer, though they can confer, and they have the option of saying that to answer that question would spoil the story. Every now and then the teacher asks who would now like to read the book, and allows the questioning to continue as long as it seems fruitful.

I've found this game to be enormously useful and usually enjoyed. An example: a group of three students read Katherine Paterson's *Bridge to Terabithia*. Their sentences went like this: 'I do not want to tell you anything about this book because it would spoil it. I think it is one of the best books I have ever read. I think you will enjoy it too, but the best way to enjoy it is just to get on and read it before you say anything about it.' My immediate reaction was that this would be the end of their turn. But not at all. There followed a long question-and-answer session as the class tried to probe what the group meant and what had made them feel as they did. Afterwards almost everyone read the book, and came back demanding a full 'Tell me' session about it because they said, having read it, they could see why the group had been so unwilling to talk about it, and now they wanted to know what everyone else thought.

Participants soon learn the questions that get the talk going like 'Where is the story set?', 'When is it set?', 'Who is the main character and what is she or he like?', 'Is it the sort of book that you can't put down?' They also learn that asking for a passage to be read aloud is helpful; and learn at the same time to rehearse a passage so as to be prepared for this request.

The educational values of this game are obvious: a book has to be read carefully enough to talk about it well; there is small-group and large-group work based on co-operative talk; a carefully constructed sentence must be written and editorial help exchanged; experience is gained of presenting thoughts, feeling, critical ideas to an audience, and of explaining and defending them; student-stimulated further reading is a possible outcome.

THE NON-READER GAME

Non-readers of a book in any group of readers are usually considered a nuisance. This is a way of making them useful. As they know nothing about the book they can be given the job of questioner and clarifier. Whenever they aren't sure what the rest of the group is talking about they must say so and the others must explain. Now and then the teacher asks them to sum up what they think has been said – and this may make the others think again about what they want to say and then express themselves more carefully and with greater subtlety.

The presence of non-readers needn't be left to chance. When selecting a book for a 'Tell me' session, a couple of people in the class can be asked not to read it and to be ready to play the part of the non-reader during the discussion. They add a little ginger to the mix.

THE RESPONSIBILITY GAME

'Make it real' should, it seems to me, be a guiding principle in all educational activity. Thus, mathematics is better learned by doing something with it that has an actual, everyday purpose than by performing exercises just to show you can do them. One of the great things about reading literature is that reading is its own 'real purpose'. You read literature for its own sake – to enjoy doing it, for the interest of the text itself, and for what may be learned from it.

Nevertheless, there are related activities involving interpretive and discriminatory procedures that, for children especially, develop their understanding of what reading means, what it is 'good for', and why they do it. The most important of these is taking responsibility for someone else's reading. There are numerous ways of doing this, but the best involve plenty of critical talk among the participants. Here are some examples, longer descriptions of which are included in Part One, *The Reading Environment*:

1. Older pupils take a selection of books to younger pupils, books they have read and discussed and think the younger ones will enjoy. And what will they do? Read aloud? In that case practice is necessary so that they can do it well. What will they say? What questions will they ask the younger ones, and which not, and why? All this needs discussion and preparation. In doing this the older pupils reflect on themselves, learn (and relearn) what kind of readers they were and are now, and make critical judgements about the value of individual books.

2. 'Have you read this?' sessions for their own class, other classes, parent groups, whoever. This again means preparing a book carefully, thinking out what you want to say about it and why it is worthwhile choosing it and encouraging others to read it. And preparing passages to read aloud.

3. Written reviews, author biographies, and other kinds of response (illustrations, cover designs, paintings of scenes, etc.) for 'publication' on display boards, school magazines, etc.

4. Anthology programmes rehearsed and presented to the whole school or to class gatherings can be extremely valuable. One of the best I've heard of involved a class of ten- and eleven-year-olds who had been enjoying the poetry of Charles Causley. They noticed that his poems can be grouped into periods of his life — his childhood, his time in the navy, his work as a teacher, and so on. They selected about ten of his poems, arranged them according to the periods of his life, wrote a linking narrative commentary, and then, after a great deal of rehearsal and editing of their script, presented this as a performance to the whole school in a programme called *Charles Causley in his Poetry*. Afterwards, the written version was bound into a book and added to the school library.

THE WORD-ASSOCIATION GAME

All literature is made of language. Anything that highlights this is useful. A simple way of getting it going is to play the word-association game with, say, a book's title. For example, ten-year-olds, not to mention some adults, often find Ted Hughes's poem 'I see a bear' a little difficult to understand. They don't know how to read it. The word-association game helps if you take each word of the first line, 'I see a bear' and look for puns and possible meanings: bear meaning an animal and a punning homonym for bare meaning naked, is a clue to the meaning of the poem as a whole; as is I, meaning me, and eye being the part of the body you see with; while see, meaning to look and to perceive, to understand, is at the heart of it too.

Always in reading it is a matter of finding patterns, of looking for connections, of keeping the mind open to possibilities.

THE QUESTIONS GAME

Doug Hilker, of the English Department at Runnymeade Collegiate Institute in Canada, suggests a 'game' that particularly suits 'Tell me' discussions of poetry but that works too with other kinds of text, especially stories and novels.

> Each student reads the poem and writes down three questions about it that he or she would like answered. Then students select a partner, try to answer each other's questions and arrive at three questions about the poem they still would like more ideas about. In the next step, two sets of partners join together in a group of four, and answer each other's questions. They settle on one question they will present for full class discussion . . .
>
> The beauty of the approach is the level of involvement by the students. They're all interested – after all, they are discussing their own questions. They all play the role of questioner and answerer. In many ways, I felt the classes went further and deeper than if I had asked all the questions. (From Frank McTeague, *Shared Reading in the Middle and High School Years*, page 52)

Hilker's conclusion, that all the students were interested and their talk went further and deeper because they were asking and answering their own questions, is at the heart of the 'Tell me' approach. 'Tell me' succeeds because it foregrounds the importance of the reader's experience of reading a text and sharing the experience of other 'similarly qualified readers' (Wayne Booth's phrase).

Endnote

I have resisted the temptation to end this book with a rhetorical flourish because the 'Tell me' approach continues to develop as more and more teachers take it up. There is no completion: it simply goes on evolving.

A great many people have contributed to 'Tell me', which began in 1980 with the study group of Steve Bicknell, Irene Suter, Barbara Raven, Jan Maxwell and Anna Collins. Where records of the work of others have been quoted, their names are gratefully acknowledged at that point.

Lissa Paul and Mary Sutcliffe commented in detail on drafts of this expanded version of the original 'Tell me' sketch that first appeared in *Booktalk.* As always, Margaret Clark gave unstinting editorial help. The revised, combined edition owes a further debt to Mary Sutcliffe and Steve Bicknell.

My thanks to them all.

References

Bracketed numbers refer to pages in the text.

W. H. Auden, 'Reading', *The Dyer's Hand and Other Essays*, Faber, 1963. [116-7, 125, 126, 131]

Wayne C. Booth, *The Company We Keep: An Ethics of Fiction*, University of California Press, 1988. [96, 162, 164, 215]

Jerome Bruner, *Actual Minds, Possible Worlds*, Harvard University Press, 1986. [51, 52, 94, 113-4]

Aidan Chambers, *Booktalk: Occasional Writing on Literature and Children* (1985), reissue, Thimble Press, 1995. [216]

Jonathan Culler, *On Deconstruction: Theory and Criticism after Structuralism*, Routledge & Kegan Paul, 1983. [116]

Richard Hoggart, 'Why I Value Literature', *About Literature*, Volume 2 of *Speaking to Each Other*, Chatto & Windus, 1970. [20]

Wolfgang Iser, *The Implied Reader: Patterns of Communication in Prose Fiction from Bunyan to Beckett*, Johns Hopkins University Press, 1974. [134]

Keith Kimberley, Margaret Meek & Jane Miller (eds), *New Readings: Contributions to an Understanding of Literacy*, A. & C. Black, 1992. [96]

David Krech, quoted in Jerome Bruner's *Actual Minds, Possible Worlds*. [20]

C.S. Lewis, *An Experiment in Criticism*, Cambridge University Press, 1961. [20]

Frank McTeague, *Shared Reading in the Middle and High School Years*, Pembroke Publications (Ontario), 1992. [214]

Margaret Mallett, 'How Long Does a Pig Live? Learning from Story and Non-Story Genres', in *New Readings: Contributions to an Understanding of Literacy*; see Kimberley, Meek & Miller above. [148-9]

Gareth B. Matthews, *Philosophy and the Young Child*, Harvard University Press, 1980. [112]

Margaret Meek, *How Texts Teach What Readers Learn*, Thimble Press, 1988. [18, 129]
Elaine Moss, '"Them's for the Infants, Miss": Some Misguided Attitudes to Picture Books for the Older Reader', part two, *Signal Approaches to Children's Books*, September 1978. [122]
Iris Murdoch, *Metaphysics as a Guide to Morals*, Chatto & Windus, 1992. [96]
Frances Clarke Sayers, *Summoned by Books*, Viking (New York), 1973. [49, 59]
Lev Vygotsky, quoted in Jerome Bruner's *Actual Minds, Possible Worlds*. [50]
Liz Waterland, *Read with Me: An Apprenticeship Approach to Reading*, second edition, Thimble Press, 1988. [50, 52]
Gordon Wells, *The Meaning Makers*, Hodder & Stoughton, 1987. [108]
John Werner, in *The Practice of English Teaching*, edited by Graham Owens & Michael Marland, Blackie, 1970. [34-5]
Maryanne Wolf, *Proust and the Squid: The Story and Science of the Reading Brain*, Icon, 2008. [62-4]